HOMESPUN DEVOTION

IDIOMS – SPIRITUALLY SPEAKING

LINDA GAINEY SMOCK

DEDICATION

There are so many people who have influenced me in my life and to whom I could dedicate this book, but after much prayer, I have settled on my parents: J.C. and Elma Gainey. Although they each left this earth many years ago, they live on in my family, and their influence on me was greater than any others, with the exception of God the Father, Jesus, and the Holy Spirit. Mom and Dad were just simple, good, hardworking country people, who saw God at work around them in their daily lives. They raised two children who have both lived their lives following the examples of their parents in many ways. They have grandchildren, great-grandchildren, and now a great-great-grandchild, and there will likely be future generations. They will continue to live on through their offspring and their influence, whether recognized or not, will continue to pass from generation to generation. Thank you, Mom and Dad. I love you.

INTRODUCTION

Growing up in the south in the mid-1900s, there were several phrases used to pass on wisdom. These colloquial sayings sometimes had roots in Biblical principles, while some had come from men like Benjamin Franklin in the Farmer's Almanac. The origins of many are vague, although we may be able to guess on some of them. For example, "Penny wise and pound foolish" sounds a lot like it has English roots.

Some have obvious origins from practices that the pilgrims and early Americans used in their daily lives. I think of "Bled like a stuck pig," and remember the fall and wintertime preparation of pigs for the smokehouse and freezer. Dad would hang the pig up by its feet, face down, and stab the neck to let the blood rush out. "He ain't got no pot to pee in," probably referred to someone who was homeless, or at least so poor that he could not afford a slop jar, kept under the bed at night for convenience in relieving oneself of urine. "Best thing since sliced bread," probably was a little later in development – after bakers started slicing bread before it was sold.

Most of these phrases are truly bits of wisdom, but sometimes they are not so true. "Don't air your dirty laundry," may not have been the best advice, since keeping family secrets was certainly not done in the Bible, nor do psychologists recommend it today.

I've found myself using these phrases over the years, passing them on to the next generations. This book will look at a few of them in light of scriptures and try to make Biblical principles come more alive for us, and easier to understand how to apply to our lives. I am not a Biblical scholar, just a sinner saved by grace, desiring to be a better disciple of Jesus. This study has helped me learn more about God the Father and Jesus, His son, and how to live a better life. That's why you will see a sentence or three in many of the devotionals about what the concept and scripture tell me about God.

You may notice that I have used many different versions of the Bible. That's purposeful. Sometimes I prefer the paraphrase over the translation; other times, I prefer the translation and want the language as close to the original as possible. I believe there is a place for all versions in our study, and that comparing them may help us understand better the concept that God wants us to learn and apply in our lives. You will find that I have used Jewish, Protestant, Catholic, old, and new – something for everyone!

Why did I write this book now? For five years, I've known that I have cancer. I was hoping the day would never come when I would need chemo, but it has, so I'm pretty much isolated in my home – not just because of the chemo, but because my immune system is extremely compromised, and there are some pretty harmful viruses and germs floating around, including the coronavirus COVID 19. So now is the time – it takes my focus off my physical problems and redirects my focus to the positive and good. It's fun, brings me joy, and puts a smile on my face. I hope it will do the same to you.

> "The only person that I need to be better than is the person I was yesterday." -Jenny Lawson

SPECIAL THANKS

My parents both transferred to heaven many years ago, but they left a part of themselves in me with the idioms they taught me and the Christian principles they practiced. Without them, these thoughts would not have developed and guided my life.

I offer my thanks to my brother, Whit Gainey, and his wife, Carol, for their guidance in my life, for their patience as I have grown and developed, and for putting up with my idiosyncrasies. I have learned a lot from both of them over the years. Their children and grandchildren are very special to me as well. I love each one of you.

I cannot name each of the ministers and teachers who have helped me over the years without missing some, but I do appreciate their help. I'd especially like to recognize Jim Shannon, Joel Singleton, and George Welty for their help in these last few years. You each have taught me a lot, and helped me love God's word even more.

Several of my friends and fellow Christians have helped me with proofing and editing as I've written. I would be amiss not to say a huge thank you to them: Barb Admire,

Sherry Chapman, Dolores Hayman, Sara Johnson, Sandy Peeples, and Kym Samek. Their input has been invaluable.

There are many, many other people who have helped me over the years – fellow teachers, neighbors, principals, even strangers. I recall a time I was mourning the death of a friend, and a Catholic priest seated next to me on a flight was able to help me see things from a fresh perspective. I never knew his name, but he was a blessing.

May these words bless all these and other people – including you.

A BIRD IN HAND IS WORTH TWO IN THE BUSH

Ecclesiastes 6:9 King James Version (KJV)
9 Better is the sight of the eyes than the wandering of the desire: this is also vanity and vexation of spirit.

Ecclesiastes 9:4 Good News Translation (GNT)
4 But anyone who is alive in the world of the living has some hope; a live dog is better off than a dead lion.

Exodus 16:13 Lexham English Bible (LEB)
13 And so it was, in the evening, the quail came up and covered the camp, and in the morning, a layer of dew was all around the camp.

This avian proverb probably started back in medieval times when falconry was so popular. One falcon on the arm was worth more than the prey it could catch that day, for it could catch prey for many days. But I think of Moses and the Israelites as they roamed in the desert for forty years. The people complained that they wanted meat, and God provided them with quail. They were easy to catch because there were so many of them. The first day that the quail appeared, the meat probably tasted wonderful after having been deprived of animal meat for a long time. One in their hands was better than two out of reach.

After over three months in isolation, other than medical appointments and outdoor walks, I'm tired of staying home. I want to make that trip I had planned with my family, and the one I had to travel to Ireland. Even a trip to the grocery store would be wonderful! But there is no COVID 19 vaccine at this point, and with my compromised immune system and chemo, I need to stay home. What is my bird in hand? I feel good. So I'm working on choosing gratitude, to be thankful for what I have, rather than focusing on what I want. Going to the grocery store, or even to church, is a considerable risk for me since my body cannot fight the virus. Home is the best place I can be! Eating the quail they had in hand instead of dreaming of the cucumbers and melons of their Egyptian slavery days was a better choice for the Israelites.

As the wise man Solomon said, "Anyone who is alive in the world of the living has some hope." I have hope – I will get to go to church, the grocery store, to visit my family, and to go to Ireland, but for now, I choose to be thankful for the good things I have.

Prayer: *Lord, being alone for so long is hard for those of us who are social people. But we have many "birds in our hands" and so much for which to be thankful. Help us make a gratitude list and be content with what we have.*

Psalm 84:3
Even the sparrow has found a home, and the swallow a nest for herself, where she may have her young— a place near Your altar, Lord Almighty, my King and my God.

HOMESPUN DEVOTION

Luke 12:6-7

Are not five sparrows sold for two pennies? Yet not one of them is forgotten by God.
Indeed, the very hairs of your head are all numbered.
Don't be afraid; you are worth more than many sparrows.

"It's a funny thing about life, once you begin to take note of the things you are grateful for, you begin to lose sight of the things that you lack." Germany Kent

NO DOG IN THAT FIGHT

> *Luke 9:49-50 The Message (MSG)*
> ⁴⁹ John spoke up, "Master, we saw a man using Your name to expel demons and we stopped him because he wasn't of our group."
>
> ⁵⁰ Jesus said, "Don't stop him. If he's not an enemy, he's an ally."

Jesus is an interesting fellow. He tells us to go and make disciples (like Him). But He also tells us not to worry if they don't believe, teach, act, or do exactly like us. Aren't you glad? Can you imagine a life where we all are the same?

John was known as one of the three best friends of Jesus, and as His very best friend, wanted "his dog in the fight." He felt as if anyone teaching or healing should be one of the few that were being personally discipled by Jesus. But Jesus refused to "put His dog in that fight." He let His best friend John know that those doing a little differently, but still proclaiming him, were not enemies, but allies.

How often we forget, and like John, we want others to agree with us – usually on things that Jesus would not "put His dog in the fight" about. Examples include the style of music used in a worship service, the place to worship (God even told David not to build a temple, that it could wait!), who can pray, and other things that are not important to Jesus or God.

What can I learn about God from this? He puts more stock in the heart of a person than in the beliefs about many things. He's not legalistic!

***Prayer:** Lord, before I argue, judge, or condemn other Christ-followers who don't see eye to eye with me, remind me that "you don't have a dog in that fight." Help me not to create fights where You would not fight.*

A DOG CHASING A FOX

> "About midnight, Paul and Silas were praying and singing hymns to God, and the other prisoners were listening to them."
> Acts 16: 25 NIV

"A dog chasing a fox does not know he has fleas." A Christian praising God doesn't think about his or her problems.

Paul sat in prison, along with Silas. Timothy and Luke sat somewhere away from the prison, wondering what was happening to Paul and Silas. Barnabas (known as "the encourager") was not there at the prison to be the encourager. Paul had spent time with him, and Paul knew how to encourage Silas and the other prisoners in that dark, crowded, stinking hole. He started to sing – perhaps a song he was familiar with, such as our songs "When Peace Like a River," or "It is Well with my Soul," or Psalm 23. Silas joined in. The other prisoners likely listened, wishing they had the peace of these men who had forgotten their troubles of flesh torn by beatings, aching muscles, and the humiliation of being stripped naked in front of a mob. The flies didn't seem as bad, and the rats didn't seem as bold.

Had Luke and Timothy learned this lesson, or were they lying awake worrying? Hopefully, they too were praising God.

No, "a dog does not know he has fleas when the chase is on," because something more important is at stake. Are you scratching the fleas or praising God? Whatever is noble, whatever is pure... think about these things.

I love this idea because it reminds me that God cares about me and my issues and wants me to face them by praising Him. He just may relieve me of them, but that's not guaranteed. However, I can be assured of the peace that comes when I adjust my attitude and praise Him with my heart.

Prayer: Heavenly Father, help me today to focus on You and Your attributes, and less on the challenges that come my way. Remind me to worship You, no matter how bad the news I hear or problems in front of me. Help me to ignore the fleas of life and focus on the goals. In Jesus's name, Amen.

"Change your thoughts and you change the world."
Norman Vincent Peale

"I am convinced that life is 10% what happens to us, and 90% how I react to it. And so it is with you... we are in charge of our attitudes." Charles Swindoll

LOOKING FOR A NEEDLE IN A HAYSTACK

Matthew 10:26-28 New Testament for Everyone (NTE)
²⁶ 'Don't be afraid of them. Nothing is hidden, you see, that won't come to light; nothing is secret that won't be made known. ²⁷ What I tell you in the dark, speak in the light, and what you hear whispered in your ears, announce from the roofs of the houses.

²⁸ 'Don't be afraid of people who can kill the body but can't kill the soul. The one you should be afraid of is the one who can destroy both body and soul in Gehenna.'

Cancer. It's a scary word. I have it, I live with it. At the time of this writing, I am undergoing chemo – but not the kind that makes folks super sick. Mine is just a pill, and yes, it has side-effects, but they are not so bad.

So how do I choose to react? Asking "Why me?" is like looking for a needle in a haystack. There really is no answer. The better question is, "Why not me?" It's so minor compared to what Jesus went through. It may feel like torture at times, but it is not torture when I consider the whips across His back, the weight of that cross, the snares set for Him in the questions, the nails in His feet and hands, and the struggle to get a breath of air... I choose chemo. I choose to meditate on "whatever is noble" and I choose to honor my Lord, no matter what comes my way.

Yes, cancer can kill the body, but not my soul. It's not cancer that I choose to fear. It's the judge of the world. My respect for Him is great, and I thank Him for the torture He allowed His son to go through so that I need not fear cancer, death, and the things of this earthly life. I have a new home waiting for me, and I can only experience it by passing through the doors of death. It will be worth it when the time comes.

These verses teach me about God. He is far more powerful than the forces common to man, and He has a plan. He wants me to be a child of light, exposing my secrets, not hiding them in a haystack. I can follow His plan to the best of my ability and live a life of peace, have a future with Him, or I can reject it and face Him as my judge.

Prayer: *Lord, give me peace as I embark on this unknown path. Lead me to choose daily to focus on the noble, the pure, not on the trials of this life. Keep me from asking "Why me?" and thus looking for "a needle in a haystack" - give me assurance that this battle is helping someone observing me. Thank You.*

Ephesians 5:11 Good News Translation (GNT)
" Have nothing to do with the worthless things that people do, things that belong to the darkness. Instead, bring them out to the light.

A STITCH IN TIME SAVES NINE

Mark 2:21-22 NIV
"No one sews a patch of unshrunk cloth on an old garment. Otherwise, the new piece will pull away from the old, making the tear worse. And no one pours new wine into old wineskins. Otherwise, the wine will burst the skins, and both the wine and the wineskins will be ruined. No, they pour new wine into new wineskins."

Romans 12:2 NIV
² Do not conform to the pattern of this world, but be transformed by the renewing of your mind. Then you will be able to test and approve what God's will is—His good, pleasing and perfect will.

Have you ever tried to sew, or seen someone try to sew, a new piece of denim on the knee of a worn-out pair of jeans? What happened the first time you (or they) wore those jeans? Pop! The worn-out threads of the old denim could not hold the strong thread of the patch. So the tear became worse. However, if a small rip occurs in a new pair of jeans and a quick repair is done, those jeans can be worn many times without further repair.

Wine today is usually put into barrels for a period of fermentation. In the old days, it was put into "wineskins." People would make containers out of fresh, clean skin, usually from a goat. They would put grape juice into one of these wineskins and close it up, and the juice would bubble and release gases until it became a beverage they wanted to drink on special occasions. The new skin was pliable and would expand and contract with the fermentation process. In contrast, if an old skin was used, it lacked that pliability and would explode as the gasses formed.

So what was the point Jesus was making? There is a common saying among businesses today: "Insanity is doing the same thing over and over and expecting different results." Keep wearing that newly ripped pair of jeans without a repair, and the tear will get bigger – you'll get the same results you got before. Keep marrying abusive spouses and you will keep getting beat up, emotionally if not physically. Keep eating beyond the calories you need for the day, and you will gain weight. Keep lying to cover things up and make yourself look good, and you'll keep getting in trouble, not being able to remember what you said to whom. "A stitch in time will save nine." Prevention is better than the pain of the consequences when we keep doing the same things.

Romans 12:2 reminds us that new ideas put into old mindsets rarely work. What we need is to renew the mind, erase the things we believe that are not true, and replace them with the truth. That means change, and we often resist it. We may choose just to keep our unchecked habits, keep doing the same things we've always done, and hope to get different results. Won't happen, Jesus says. Paul agrees.

Reading these scriptures reminds me that God has a plan, a will – and that mixing the old and the new doesn't work well. He tells me how to change – renew my mind, which means I have to stop believing the lies I've based previous decisions on. I have to work at it, however. The good news: He'll hold my hand through the process. All I have to do is study the New Testament characters, and I see how He held their hands through their change process: John went from being the Son of Thunder to a man who wrote much about love and self-control. Peter was so afraid that he lied three times about knowing Jesus, and later preached a powerful sermon that set the stage for Christianity. Paul had to be changed from the Saul who hated Christians and would persecute and execute them, to the chief spokesperson for Christians.

__Prayer:__ Father of the ultimate plan, hold my hand as I strive to change some habits and some habitual ways of thinking that are not the best for me. Renew my mind. Help me put "a stitch in time to save nine." I realize that doing things just like I've always done will only lead to the same results. I trust You to prod me back on track when I wander off.

"Even when things seem to be going wrong, they just could be going right because you're in God's will, the negatives are part of His positive program." Tony Evans

A WATCHED POT NEVER BOILS

Luke 15:20 The Voice (VOICE)
[20] So he got up and returned to his father. The father looked off in the distance and saw the young man returning. He felt compassion for his son and ran out to him, enfolded him in an embrace, and kissed him.

Suggested reading: Luke 15:11-32

Waiting. I am not fond of it and I'm guessing you are not a fan either. We wait in line at the grocery store, for sports and entertainment events, and for the bathroom. We wait for news from the doctor. We wait for news about the weather. We wait for news from loved ones who are traveling, in the armed services, or in the hospital.

We wait. Just like this father waited for his son, we wait with hope, but sometimes with fear and worry as well. We don't know how to feel, don't know how to wait. This father was watching...not just wishing, not just hoping, not just coping but actually watching with faith he'd see his son again. Perhaps the dad had been young and foolish and he possibly knew from experience what was likely to happen. He probably knew it when Junior went off to spend that money on women, wine, and song. But he never gave up hope – faith!

When I am waiting for the pot to boil, where is my faith? Am I worrying as I watch? Am I praying as I watch? Is my faith in God such that I can accept the outcome, whether the results are what I want or not? Have I asked God to prepare me for the answer, especially if it's not what I want? Have I surrendered the timetable to God, feeling at peace that His timing is better than mine? Do I walk away, trusting the pot will be boiling when I return?

Eventually, that watched pot will boil. Patience, perseverance, humility – fruits of the Spirit are being developed in my life as I wait. It's worth it.

What does this tell me about God? He's not just waiting. He's watching for you and me. His arms of welcome are open. He cares, and He welcomes us when we come.

Prayer: *Thank You, dear God in heaven, for such love – love that You watch as You wait, wanting me to run to You. Your arms are open. Help me surrender and come, just as I am, to watch the pots of my life with faith that You will bring them to boil at just the perfect time.*

"Change will not come if we wait for some other person or some other time. We are the ones we've been waiting for. We are the change we seek." Barack Obama

"I believe that a trusting attitude and a patient attitude go hand in hand. You see, when you let go and learn to trust God, it releases joy in your life. And when you trust God, you're able to be more patient. Patience is not just about waiting for something… it's about how you wait, or your attitude while waiting." Joyce Myer

ADD A LITTLE WATER TO THE SOUP

Romans 12:10-14 New International Version (NIV)
[10] Be devoted to one another in love. Honor one another above yourselves. [11] Never be lacking in zeal, but keep your spiritual fervor, serving the Lord. [12] Be joyful in hope, patient in affliction, faithful in prayer. [13] Share with the Lord's people who are in need. Practice hospitality.

[14] Bless those who persecute you; bless and do not curse.
[15] Rejoice with those who rejoice; mourn with those who mourn.

Hebrews 13:1-2 Holman Christian Standard Bible (HCSB)
[13] Let brotherly love continue. [2] Don't neglect to show hospitality, for by doing this some have welcomed angels as guests without knowing it.

Suggested reading: Mark 2:13-17 and John 8:1-11

When I was a child, in the panhandle of Florida, almost every Sunday after church services, I heard the phrase, "Ya'll come on over, we'll add a little water to the soup." It was a tradition in my little farming community: every Sunday, somebody went to someone else's home for dinner but mostly to spend time together, talking, and relaxing. The menu was not as important as the relationships.

When I look at the life of Jesus, I see a life of hospitality, but not in the way we Americans do hospitality. No, Martha Stewart had not influenced Him, there was no HGTV or Food Network, and expectations were simple. When His mother, Mary, asked Him to provide wine for a wedding reception, He prevented the host from being embarrassed and running out of wine. And when the little man Zacchaeus came down from the tree, Jesus suggested that they dine together (Luke 19). I don't think for a moment that Jesus was looking for a free meal, but I do think He was seeking to create real connections between people, and modeling for us what we are to do, just as Paul admonished us to do in Romans 12:10-14. In Mark 2:13-17, Jesus was criticized by the religious leaders for eating with "sinners." (Who else could He eat with? Isn't everyone a sinner?) He didn't care. He wanted good relationships with all kinds of people. I can only imagine whom He would invite to come to a banquet He hosted: Muslims, Buddhists, monks, drunks, priests, drug dealers, royalty, the poorest people in the city, celebrities, taxi drivers, custodians, transgender people, preachers, and the list goes on. He was not and is not looking at what we are, but what we can become. He cares for each of us just as we are, where we are. While He is the ultimate judge, His response to our sins is the same as it was to the woman caught in adultery: "I don't condemn you. Go your way and leave your life of sin." (See John 8:1-11 for this story.)

He still invites us to eat at His table. Everybody. No matter what you believe, where you've been or where you are going. He'll "add a little water to the soup," and welcome you, me, and all those we tend to exclude.

HOMESPUN DEVOTION

Prayer: *Lord, my invitations tend to be for people like me, not people who are different or don't have the same basic beliefs and values I have. Help me learn to practice hospitality in the way You would have me practice it, with a heart and mind open to accepting and loving people who are not like me. Show me when I need to "add a little water to the soup," extend a helping hand, and a hopeful heart. Thank You.*

"There are no strangers here; only friends you have not met yet."
William Butler Yeats

"If we have no peace, it is because we have forgotten we belong to each other."
Mother Teresa

"A single conversation across the table with a wise man is better than ten years with mere study of books."
Henry Wadsworth Longfellow

"You can't change the world if you can't change yourself."
Titus O'Neil

ADDING FUEL TO THE FIRE OR DOUSING THE FIRE?

2 Chronicles 7:14 Revised Standard Version (RSV)
¹⁴ if my people who are called by my name humble themselves, and pray and seek my face, and turn from their wicked ways, then I will hear from heaven, and will forgive their sin and heal their land.

Psalm 4:3 Revised Standard Version (RSV)
³ But know that the L<small>ORD</small> has set apart the godly for Himself; the L<small>ORD</small> hears when I call to Him.

I love the good 'ole USA – but I'm not in denial. There are problems. Well, PROBLEMS.

We have: Problems with social injustice, problems with a few police officers, problems with lack of respect for law enforcement, problems with lack of respect for people who look different, problems within our government, and problems outside our government. Most of all, we have problems within our hearts, with not loving God, and with not loving our neighbors as ourselves.

Am I adding fuel to the fire? Or am I dousing the fire?

When Solomon finished building the temple, God talked with him. One of the things God told him was that the people needed to pray, to turn from their wicked ways, and to seek Him. I wonder if He is trying to tell us the same thing, and specifically, to stop fueling the fire by posting things on social media condemning certain persons, cultures, political parties, careers, and other things we don't like. Instead of these choices, I think He may be telling us to pray for all people, cultures, political parties and their politicians and appointed officials. Healing comes after prayer. Hatred is not healthy. It builds up inside of us and leads to riots, burning of buildings, looting of businesses, killing of people, and other forms of harm to the human race.

David tells us in Psalm 4 that God hears our prayers. Sometimes, we don't feel like He does, because we don't get the answer we want, or because His timing is not our timing. But He does.

So let's pray. Let's pray that the social injustices are corrected, that law authorities can do their jobs right and well, that we respect our elected and appointed leaders enough to pray for them, and that we submit to God's will, not try to force our will on God or on the people around us or those following our social media postings. Let's pray and act by using our social media posts to help our nation heal, not further split it. Let's douse the fire with the healing waters of God's love!

Prayer: *Dear God of this United States of America, You and You alone know the past and the future perfectly. You have a* *plan for what is in place and for what is to come. You use the current circumstances, no matter how bad they are, to create win-wins in the future. You tell us this in Romans 8:28, and You show it to us by Your actions, over and over. Our trust is in You, not social media. Keep me, my friends, and my loved ones from adding fuel to the fire. Teach us to douse the fire of anger.*

Philippians 4:8-10 New Revised Standard Version Catholic Edition (NRSVCE)
⁸ Finally, beloved, whatever is true, whatever is honorable, whatever is just, whatever is pure, whatever is pleasing, whatever is commendable, if there is any excellence and if there is anything worthy of praise, think about these things. ⁹ Keep on doing the things that you have learned and received and heard and seen in me, and the God of peace will be with you.

Matthew 7:12 New Testament for Everyone
So whatever you want people to do to you, do just that to them. Yes; this is what the law and the prophets are all about.

"Returning hate for hate multiplies hate, adding deeper darkness to a night already devoid of stars. Darkness cannot drive out darkness; only light can do that. Hate cannot drive out hate, only love can do that."
Martin Luther King

Titus 3:1-2 ESV
Remind them to be submissive to rulers and authorities, to be obedient, to be ready for every good work, to speak evil of no one, to avoid quarreling, to be gentle, and to show perfect courtesy toward all people.

HOMESPUN DEVOTION

I Timothy 2:1-2 ESV

First of all, then, I urge that supplications, prayers, intercessions, and thanksgiving be made for all people, for kings and all who are in high positions, that we may lead a peaceful and quiet life, Godly and dignified in every way.

DON'T AIR YOUR DIRTY LAUNDRY...

John 4:39-42 The Message
Many of the Samaritans from that village committed themselves to Him because of the woman's witness: "He knew all about the things I did. He knows me inside and out!" They asked Him to stay on, so Jesus stayed two days. A lot more people entrusted their lives to Him when they heard what He had to say. They said to the woman, "We're no longer taking this on your say-so. We've heard it for ourselves and know it for sure. He's the Savior of the world!"

Ephesians 5:13 NIV
[13] But everything exposed by the light becomes visible—and everything that is illuminated becomes a light.

Suggested Reading: John 4:1-35 and Psalm 51

"Don't air your dirty laundry." I've heard this phrase all my life, meaning that it is best not to share our family's secrets. But is that wise? Jesus exposed the secrets the Samaritan woman was trying to hide from the world, and He gave her freedom and peace as a result. Can we also have freedom when we share our "dirty laundry?"

In Psalm 51, David does not specifically name his sin, but he admits sin, and how bad he has been (verses 1-3). Was this necessary for him to have freedom from guilt? Probably so. He had to come clean with God to feel forgiveness. He had to call his sin, "sin" – name it and claim it.

Think of Alcoholics Anonymous. Meetings start with "My name is _____, and I'm an alcoholic." Why? To air the dirty laundry! To name the sin! Tell Jesus (He already knows it), tell a trusted friend, counselor, support group... Getting it off your chest can help you find freedom and peace.

What does this tell me about God? He welcomes us to air our dirty laundry with Him – and He changes the darkness that it creates into light!

Prayer: *Lord, help me know to whom to air my dirty laundry. Help me have confidence I can freely share with You. Let peace attend my soul and mind as You change darkness into light. You already know why I feel guilty, and You've already said You would take my guilt for me. Thank You. But God, sometimes I need help to let it go, to leave it at Your feet. I give it to You, but sometimes I take it back. Don't let me! Please remind me it is yours now.*

"To err is human, to forgive, divine." Alexander Pope

AS HANDY AS A POCKET ON A SHIRT

Philippians 4:8 NIV
Finally, brothers, whatever is true, whatever is noble, whatever is right, whatever is pure, whatever is lovely, whatever is admirable – if anything is excellent or praiseworthy, think about such things.

Suggested reading: Philippians 4:4-9

There are many idioms similar to this one but "handy as a pencil" is equally popular. Both mean that it helps to have you around, or that it is good to have the convenience of a tool, appliance, or other resource.

If there was a way to video or audio tape our minds and play it back for our family and friends to see, what would they observe and hear? Would it be noble? Would it be pure? Would it be admirable, or even righteous?

Many authors teach that one way to train our minds to think on the pure and noble is to purposefully begin to list attributes of God, and things for which we are thankful, using the alphabet as our guide. It is easy to find ourselves worrying, focusing on ungodly things, or being pulled toward bad habits such as over-shopping, too much TV, or substance abuse.. The alphabet exercise can refocus our minds to noble and pure things. For example, God is awesome, beautiful, creative, divine, eternal, forgiving, generous, holy, etc. Another great tool is to pray the Lord's prayer (Matthew 6:9-15), making it personal to our situation. Praying scriptures is a third tool that is very helpful in redirecting our minds off our troubles.

As we make snapshots and tapes of our minds today, let's redirect our thoughts to focus on the noble, the righteous, the pure. They will be as "handy as a pocket on a shirt."

These verses tell me that God's mind is on the pure and noble. That's where He wants mine also.

Prayer: Heavenly Father, Noble and Pure One, guide my thought patterns today and every day that You may be glorified. Help me to develop godly habits of my mind that I may never be ashamed for You to see or hear what is in my mind. Keep those good habits "as handy as a pocket on a shirt."

BAD COMPANY CORRUPTS GOOD MORALS

Proverbs 1:10-14 The Passion Translation (TPT)

*[10] When peer pressure compels you to go with the crowd
and sinners invite you to join in,
you must simply say, "No!"
[11] When the gang says—
"We're going to steal and kill and get away with it.
[12] We'll take down the rich and rob them.
We'll swallow them up alive and take what we want from whomever we want.
[13] Then we'll take their treasures and fill our homes with loot.
[14] So come on and join us.
Take your chance with us.
We'll divide up all we get;
we'll each end up with big bags of cash!"*

Peer pressure. We hear the phrase frequently. All of us have peer pressure, and as adults, we're aware that younger people are most susceptible. That is the time when we are most likely to give in to illegal activities such as stealing, drugs, underage drinking, etc.

But as adults, don't we all give in to peer pressure? Have you ever eaten something when your stomach was full, but you ate it just to please another person? Or have you nodded in seeming agreement with someone when you really didn't agree with their statement? I have a friend who went parasailing to please her family – and hated every minute of it! Yes, we give in to peer pressure too.

Why do we people please? Probably most of us do it when we feel insecure. We don't stop to realize it, but we make decisions based on what others want us to do, not what we want to do. We want them to be happy, so we neglect our own needs. We don't like conflict. Peace at any cost is worth giving up our own desires. If we stop and think about it, it's better to have conflict, and risk not having peace, than to do whatever it is the person wants from us, especially if it is illegal or immoral. We need to think about the wisdom of doing or not doing whatever it is and make a decision based on what is best, right, and pleasing to God.

Simply say "No." That's what the wise man Solomon had to say about peer pressure. Taking chances is foolish and adds to our distress. Oh, it may seem fun at the moment, but following it, we regret it. God indicates in this scripture that He wants us to use wisdom, not to "follow the crowd." But God doesn't make us do what He advises. He gives us free choice. That empowers me to do what I choose – and I hope I choose to use wisdom in most cases. That's what God wants, and He even promises to make His wisdom available to us! (See James 1:5)

Prayer: *Father, it is so tempting to give in to what others expect of me. But it is not wise in so many cases. Help me quickly weigh each opportunity, and not give in unless it is the wise and godly thing to do. Give me peace in my heart even if there is no peace between the other person and me. Don't let my morals be corrupted by the desires of others. Thank You.*

Galatians 1:10 The Living Bible (TLB)
[10] You can see that I am not trying to please you by sweet talk and flattery; no, I am trying to please God. If I were still trying to please men I could not be Christ's servant.

Proverbs 29:25 The Living Bible (TLB)
[25] Fear of man is a dangerous trap, but to trust in God means safety.

1 Thessalonians 2:4 New International Version (NIV)
[4] On the contrary, we speak as those approved by God to be entrusted with the gospel. We are not trying to please people but God, who tests our hearts.

BLESS YOUR HEART

Psalm 34:8 Lexham English Bible (LEB)
⁸ Taste and see that Yahweh is good;
blessed is the man who takes refuge in Him.

This morning, I woke up early, so I took a hot beverage down to the porch at the end of my condo building wing and sat down, taking in the beauty and sounds of the early morning, with my heart being blessed with each sight and sound. The whippoorwills were saying good night in the woods across the lake, and the limpkins were calling their mates. The sun was not visible, but was reflecting on the clouds, creating a red hue. On my side of the lake, a few bats were sailing past, grabbing a few breakfast mosquitoes before heading for their roost. A heron rose up and flew over me, and moorhens began to call their young. Soon, the redwing blackbirds were chatting away, and the mockingbirds began to sing. A neighborhood cat sauntered by, looking for a place to cross the fence, too lazy or perhaps too tired to climb it. Crows began to chime in. The crickets quieted down. Soon, the sky was bright with the morning light.

Yes, my heart was blessed. I was refreshed, ready for the day. I had tasted and seen that Yahweh is good. But as I walked back to my condo, I thought of how many ways the phrase, "Bless your heart" is used. Likely, you have heard it used to soften the blow of an insult. It's also used as pity, as sympathy, and as a heartfelt expression of concern. I've used it, I'm afraid, because I wanted to be sweet and kind, and not say something like, "You stupid idiot, of course that happened to you – it's your own fault."

Because I've heard it used so often, and probably been guilty myself, to soften the coming insult, I have almost ceased using the phrase, choosing instead, "May God bless you." May I suggest that we may add asking God to bless them in a specific way, such as with peace, with adequate food for the week, with healing, or better health. There are so many ways we can be specific in a prayer, and then we don't have to be concerned about how the person will take the phrase, especially if it has been used in their home or work environment as an insult. What's more, most of us don't want pity. We want support and help. By asking Yahweh (God) to bless them in a specific way, the person can feel supported and comforted. It is a prayer, offering us and the person refuge in the shelter of God's wings. That leads to true blessings to the heart.

What do I learn about God as I ponder on this? I learn that He wants us to take refuge in Him and run to Him to find relief. He cares, and He will bless our hearts in little ways and big ways.

Prayer: Lord, bring to my mind any times that I have misused this phrase, and help me to ask that person's forgiveness and seek Your forgiveness. You are faithful, and You will answer. I also ask that You help me break the habit of using the phrase that so often causes others to be hurt. Help me replace it with genuine responses that are honest and caring. Thank You.

Psalm 143:8 NIV
"Let the morning bring me word of your unfailing love, for I have put my trust in You."

BARKING UP THE WRONG TREE

Acts 8:3 The Message (MSG)

³*And Saul just went wild, devastating the church, entering house after house after house, dragging men and women off to jail.*

Acts 9:5-6 The Message (MSG)

⁵⁻⁶ *He said, "Who are You, Master?"*
"I am Jesus, the One you're hunting down. I want you to get up and enter the city. In the city you'll be told what to do next."

Computers. Technology. They are so tiring to try to figure out for many of us who are older and who didn't start off using them until middle age or beyond, yet so important to our daily functioning.

I tried to install a new printer recently but gave up and called for remote help (all that is available during the COVID-19 pandemic)! We worked together, doing what we thought the instructions were telling us to do, but to no avail. We could scan, but not print. Finally, we started over, and found that the computer thought it was the old printer that we wanted to print to. Duh. "Barking up the wrong tree." (And the good news here, the computer sage did not charge me for the time he was "barking up the wrong tree!")

It made me think of Saul turned Paul, a man who wrote much of the New Testament. If you attended Sunday school as a child, it is very likely that you know a little about his story. He "barked up the wrong tree."

Paul was convinced that Jesus was a fraud. He was convinced that His followers were "two bricks shy of a load." So he sincerely went about having them arrested, thrown into prison, and even stoned to death.

Until...

Suddenly, while he was traveling down the road, a bright light blinded him, and he heard a voice speak. He asked about it, and the answer was basically, "This is Jesus, the one you are fighting so hard."

Paul: "You mean You are for real? But that can't be!"

Jesus: "I'm real. I died on that cross, and I was resurrected. I'm in heaven with God now, and I want you to be the man who leads the church into the next steps. You're my man."

So Paul obeyed. You can read the story in Acts 8 and 9. He went through quite a transformation, became a new man in many ways, and was a great disciple and apostle for Jesus, leading the early church in spiritual growth like no other man in history.

Like Paul, and like my computer tech, we need to admit it when we've barked up the wrong tree. There is nothing wrong with changing our mind and beginning anew. In fact, it can be quite refreshing, as we are transformed into people after God's own heart of love.

What do I learn about God in this passage? I learn that He cares, that He gives fresh starts, that He is full of mercy and grace, willing to work with me to help me become fresh, renewed, and full of mercy and grace. He will empower me to become like Him, to find Him, and bark up His tree!

> ***Prayer:*** *Lord, when I "bark up the wrong tree," show me clearly, and help me be honest about it so I can change, be transformed, by truth – whether it's a life issue, a spiritual issue, or as simple as a computer issue. Thank You.*

"When she transformed into a butterfly, the caterpillars spoke not of her beauty, but of her weirdness. They wanted her to change back into what she always had been. But she had wings." Dean Jackson

"Practice is the hardest part of learning, and training is the essence of transformation." Ann Voskamp

BEGGARS CAN'T BE CHOOSERS

Philippians 4:11-12 New International Version (NIV)
¹¹ I am not saying this because I am in need, for I have learned to be content whatever the circumstances. ¹² I know what it is to be in need, and I know what it is to have plenty. I have learned the secret of being content in any and every situation, whether well fed or hungry, whether living in plenty or in want.

I am isolated as I write this. The pandemic for the coronavirus COVID-19 is all around, and I have a compromised immune system. I can choose to do as the doctor says and be isolated, or I can choose to go out in public, in which case I risk getting an infection, whether or not it is COVID-19. I don't like being sick, so I choose isolation. I was isolated before the COVID-19 scare started, but COVID has definitely extended it, made things I can go out for fewer.

When I have needs, I am dependent on others to assist me – prescriptions, groceries, etc. I've been super independent all my life, and being dependent on others and asking for help is not easy. I choose it over being sick, however. Recently, when I was in need of paper towels, I asked a friend to pick some up for me, if they were available (paper towels and toilet paper have been bought by those hoarding, making the store shelves empty). She asked my preference, and I said, "Bounty, solid white." Then I added, "But beggars can't be choosers. Get whatever they have." Incidentally, they had none, so she was unable to get any brand at all.

Another choice I have is whether to be angry and upset that I can no longer be independent, unable to take care of what seem like basic needs. I can choose to dwell on my circumstances and have a pity party. Or I can do like Paul – choose to be content in the circumstances I am in. That's my current choice, although I do occasionally fight that pity party. In choosing to be content, I am choosing a joyful life, as well as trusting God to teach me as I go through this time of isolation. As a social butterfly, learning to be content in these circumstances is an important lesson. I am blessed in thousands of ways, and so, contentment in isolation can be added to my blessings.

What does this teach me about God? Since His instruction is "Be content," I believe that God wants what is best for me and knows that contentment in bad situations makes them easier to deal with.

Prayer: *Lord, it's true. "Beggars can't be choosers." They have to take what they can get. Help me get through the times of need with an attitude of contentment, to look to You to teach me, to smile with joy whether I have all I want or not. Thank You for filling my heart with love for You and thus leading me to be content, whatever the circumstances.*

"Sometimes it's the smallest decisions that can change your life forever."
Keri Russell

"Anything is possible when you have the right people there to support you." Misty Copeland

"Many people will walk in and out of your life, but only true friends will leave footprints in your heart." Eleanor Roosevelt

BOTH CUT FROM SAME BOLT OF CLOTH

Luke 15:11, 28-29 The Voice (VOICE)
¹¹ Once there was this man who had two sons. ¹² One day the younger son came to his father and said, "Father, eventually I'm going to inherit my share of your estate. Rather than waiting until you die, I want you to give me my share now."

²⁸ The older brother got really angry and refused to come inside, so his father came out and pleaded with him to join the celebration. ²⁹ But he argued back, "Listen, all these years I've worked hard for you. I've never disobeyed one of your orders. But how many times have you even given me a little goat to roast for a party with my friends? Not once! <u>This is not fair!</u>

Suggested reading: Luke 15:11-32

If you are a parent, or a teacher, an uncle, an aunt, or a grandparent, you've heard the phrase: That's not fair! And it well may not be. We want what we think we deserve, and sometimes we go to extremes to get it. Perhaps these two boys in the story, that most of us know as the prodigal son, were "cut from the same bolt of cloth" – the fabric of selfishness.

The first one made his selfishness evident: "Give me what I want," he said to his dad. "I want money, and I don't care if you have to sell some of your assets to get it for me." The dad, probably reluctantly, gave in, and did as his son wanted. He likely understood, because he may have done something similar in his youth.

The second one worked hard, not expressing and even actively hiding his desire, but believing he would be greatly rewarded for his hard work and dedication. When his little brother came home, broken, ashamed, embarrassed, and humbled, he got angry – because the dad was throwing a celebration party. His selfishness came out and became evident to all. And like all of us did as children, he yelled, "That's not fair!" He was right, it wasn't, but it was deserved, because humility is more important than fairness. Humility is the attitude that leads us to admit what we've done wrong, to surrender to God, and leave it to Him whether or not the situation is righted.

What brings out my selfishness? When am I thinking, "That's not fair," even if I don't say it? How do I go about manipulating and trying to get my own way? The answers to these questions can help me grow in spiritual gifts, leading me to a more fulfilled life. There is nothing selfish about God, who allowed His son to come to earth, die, and be resurrected for me and for you. It was not fair, not what Jesus deserved. But God's love for me trumped, and death led to victory for both Jesus and me. That's love, grace, and mercy all wrapped in one. I'd rather have those than fairness.

Prayer: *Father and Daddy of us prodigals, I come to You acknowledging that I am a selfish human, wanting what I want when I want it, manipulating at times to get my own way. Forgive me, show me clearly when I do, lead me so I can grow in You, putting You and others ahead of my selfish desires. Recut me from a new bolt of cloth, the one from which You cut Jesus. Thank You.*

"The remarkable thing is, we have a choice everyday regarding the attitude we will embrace for that day."
Charles R. Swindoll

"Success is not what you have done compared to what others have done. Success is what you have done compared to what you were supposed to do." Tony Evans

BY HOOK OR CROOK

1 Corinthians 16:13 Common English Bible (CEB)
¹³ Stay awake, stand firm in your faith, be brave, be strong.

2 Chronicles 20:17 Complete Jewish Bible (CJB)
¹⁷ You won't even need to fight this battle! Just take your positions, Y'hudah and Yerushalayim, stand still, and watch how A<small>DONAI</small> will deliver you! Don't be afraid or distressed; tomorrow, go out against them; for A<small>DONAI</small> is with you.'"

2 Corinthians 12:10 Complete Jewish Bible (CJB)
¹⁰ Yes, I am well pleased with weaknesses, insults, hardships, persecutions and difficulties endured on behalf of the Messiah; for it is when I am weak that I am strong.

"By hook or by crook" sounds like an honest and a dishonest way of getting what you want! If you can't get it legally, you can go for it illegally. But that's not the history. The phrase was used in as early as 1380, by John Wycliff, when he referred to a shepherd's staff, used to pull wayward sheep back into the flock or back to the shepherd. The "hook" likely referred to an agricultural tool used to cut grass, corn, and other grains. It was shaped with a curved, sharp blade on a short handle. Both were honest forms of determination.

The crook could also refer to the guideline back in that time which allowed people to take firewood that they could reach with their "crook," even if it was on another man's property. Ernest Hemingway used the phrase in a short story and made it popular again. It was also the name of a movie in 2001.

Basically, it's about determination, getting what is needed by whatever means we have available. That takes faith, and often requires courage, bravery, and strength. Yet faith seems to be the most important aspect, because we have to believe it is possible to have the determination to go for it. Today, we might say, "I'm going to go to Alaska by hook or by crook" indicating that we are determined to go, no matter what.

When I was four or five years old, a teacher at the school in town (I lived in the country) brought her boys to our farm to pick cotton. She wanted them to have the experience. She sat on our front porch with me in her lap, and I believe she read to me. She definitely talked to me. I decided that day that I wanted to be a teacher when I grew up, "by hook or by crook!" When I started school in first grade, she was my teacher, and I was thrilled!

But to become a teacher meant I had to go to college – not something common in my family. Only one cousin had ever gone to college, and there were lots of cousins. (I was the "baby" on my dad's side and one of the younger ones on my mother's side.) I was determined. There were times it felt hopeless, but I never gave up. I became a teacher, and later a curriculum supervisor, a textbook author, and a principal. It was that "by hook or crook" attitude that got me through college and into the classroom. After 44 years, I retired, but I still volunteer to teach! I'm so thankful that faith and determination got me through thick and thin, and I was able to achieve my goal.

My faith was not just in myself, however. I had faith in my parents to support me, faith in my teachers to guide me, and most importantly, faith in God to provide the determination, strength, and courage I needed for each step along the way. It's like Paul says in his second letter to the Corinthians, God is pleased when I admit my weaknesses and rely on Him. He can get me through challenges and difficulties, but He does ask me to have faith in Him. That faith then leads to courage and strength. God is strong and has courage. He willingly shares, and all I need to do is ask and submit.

> **Prayer:** *God of Joshua, whom You told to be "strong and courageous" – I need Your help to also be strong and courageous as I face the various situations in my life that take determination. Help me, "by hook or crook," to look to You in faith so that I can attain the goals that I need to reach throughout each phase of life. When I am weak, You are strong, and You can make me strong enough for the task at hand.*

Joshua 1:7-8 Lexham English Bible (LEB)
⁷ Only be strong and very courageous *to observe diligently the whole law* that Moses my servant commanded you. Do not turn aside from it, *to* the right or left, so that you may succeed *wherever you go.* ⁸ The scroll of this law will not depart from your mouth; you will meditate on it day and

night so that *you may observe diligently all that is written* in it. For then you will succeed *in* your ways and prosper.

Hebrews 11:1 King James Version (KJV)
Now faith is the substance of things hoped for, the evidence of things not seen.

"A determined person will do more with a pen and paper, than a lazy person will accomplish with a personal computer." Catherine Pulsifer

BY THE SKIN OF HIS TEETH

Colossians 2:13-15 The Message (MSG)
11-15 Entering into this fullness is not something you figure out or achieve. It's not a matter of being circumcised or keeping a long list of laws. No, you're already in—insiders—not through some secretive initiation rite but rather through what Christ has already gone through for you, destroying the power of sin. If it's an initiation ritual you're after, you've already been through it by submitting to baptism. Going under the water was a burial of your old life; coming up out of it was a resurrection, God raising you from the dead as He did Christ. When you were stuck in your old sin-dead life, you were incapable of responding to God. God brought you alive—right along with Christ! Think of it! All sins forgiven, the slate wiped clean, that old arrest warrant canceled and nailed to Christ's cross. He stripped all the spiritual tyrants in the universe of their sham authority at the Cross and marched them naked through the streets.

When I was in junior college (are there still such things?), President Kennedy put out a challenge for physical fitness. My PE teacher followed the guidelines, and we were all to be tested in certain things, and one of them was the distance jump. I was not good, so I decided to practice. The grass just below the doorsteps of our country home was an easy place to know my starting place, so I marked it, jumped, and got down on hands and knees to measure. "Hisssss" I heard, and looked straight into the eyes of a cottonmouth moccasin! I jumped backwards, but I didn't measure it – could have been my record jump of the season! Missed danger "by the skin of my teeth..."

If you are like me, there have been some narrow escapes in your life – perhaps an almost auto accident, a financial mistake, a close encounter with a dangerous creature or person, or a health issue. You may have said, "missed that by the skin of my teeth." We feel like it was a miracle we escaped, because it was so close! Yet we know full well, teeth don't have skin!

We as Christians are missing damnation by the skin of our teeth – or better said, by the blood of Jesus. If it takes perfection to go to heaven, then we can't do it. We make mistakes. I do, daily. But thankfully, I don't have to worry. Jesus will say to God, "I've got her covered. My blood sacrifice by my death on the cross takes care of her because she believed in me, tried to follow me. No, she didn't keep the letter of the law, and no, she didn't figure out everything I tried to teach her, but her mistakes are blotted out, her slate is clean. Let her into heaven." Those will be wonderful words to hear, and they give me peace on this earth as I prepare to transition to that next life.

What do I learn about God as I read this scripture? I learn that God loves me so much that He created a plan to make me the imperfect perfect so I can get into heaven. We call it grace.

Prayer: *Lord Jesus, but for Your sacrifice, I would miss heaven by miles, but because of Your death, the flowing out of Your blood for me, and Your resurrection, I will be let in. I don't have to worry about a narrow escape from damnation because You have given Your grace to cover my messy life. Thank You.*

Romans 8:30-33 Living Bible (TLB)
[30] And having chosen us, He called us to come to Him; and when we came, He declared us "not guilty," filled us with Christ's goodness, gave us right standing with himself, and promised us His glory.

[31] What can we ever say to such wonderful things as these? If God is on our side, who can ever be against us? [32] Since He did not spare even His own Son for us but gave Him up for us all, won't He also surely give us everything else?

[33] Who dares accuse us whom God has chosen for His own? Will God? No! He is the one who has forgiven us and given us right standing with himself.

CAST THE NET WIDER

John 21:4-8 Tree of Life Version (TLV)
⁴ At dawn, Yeshua stood on the beach; but the disciples didn't know that it was Yeshua. ⁵ So Yeshua said to them, "Boys, you don't happen to have any fish, do you?"

"No," they answered Him.

⁶ He said to them, "Throw the net off the right side of the boat, and you'll find some." So they threw the net, and they were not able to haul it in because of the great number of fish.

⁷ Therefore the disciple whom Yeshua loved said to Peter, "It's the Lord!" When Simon Peter heard that it was the Lord, he tied his outer garment around himself—for he was stripped down for work—and threw himself into the sea. ⁸ But the other disciples came in the boat from about two hundred cubits[a] offshore, dragging the net full of fish.

"Cast the net wider" is a phrase often used in the business world, especially when looking for the right person for a job opening. The applicants on hand don't seem to be the right catch, so efforts are made to "cast the net wider."

We may also "cast the net wider" when we are looking for that perfect piece of furniture, or perhaps the right suit or dress for a special occasion. We keep looking.

The same is true for many folks when it comes to their spiritual beliefs. They may try one religion, then another, and another, and another... hoping to find peace or satisfaction.

John and Peter had given up on Jesus and gone back to fishing. They had been so completely enamored with Jesus that they were ready to follow Him and do whatever He said. They were convinced that He would be king of the Jews and rescue Israel from the cruelty of the Roman government. But then, He died, a horrible death of crucifixion. They were not ready to cast the net wider, they were just ready to give up and go back to their comfort zone – fishing. But then a stranger showed up and suggested they cast their net on the other side of the boat. Since they had nothing to lose, they did so. That stranger was right – they caught fish! More than they knew what to do with! And suddenly, John realized that the stranger was the man he believed to be dead – Jesus. He told Peter, who quickly got dressed, shamed by his state of undress there in the lake. From that point until their deaths, they followed Jesus. No more fish net casting. They knew this was the son of God, worthy of being followed. Their lives were no longer limited to a local friendship group. Jesus cast His vision – the new idea/new net of fishing for men. Following a leader who yet again left them as He ascended to heaven, they were obedient, followed His teachings, and spread the news about Him. There were consequences to stepping into Jesus's net – years later, Peter was even beheaded for being an obedient follower – but the important thing was stepping into that net with fervor until the end of this side of life.

This scripture reminds me that God doesn't give up on us, and He will cast His net toward me until I surrender. His net will come my way, but it's my choice whether I decide to jump into it.

***Prayer:** Lord, I need Your help daily to recognize You and Your works so that I surrender more fully to them. Help me limit my net-casting to the areas You want me to cast in. Lead me to throw to the side of the boat where the results are orchestrated by You. And when You are casting the net toward me, help me jump in so that I can more fully align myself with Your values, Your ways, Your will.*

DON'T COUNT YOUR CHICKS BEFORE THEY HATCH

Luke 12:18-20 The Voice (VOICE)
¹⁸ I know! I'll tear down my small barns and build even bigger ones, and then I'll have plenty of storage space for my grain and all my other goods. ¹⁹ Then I'll be able to say to myself, 'I have it made! I can relax and take it easy for years! So I'll just sit back, eat, drink, and have a good time!'"

Have you ever hatched eggs? If so, whether the hen sat on them to keep them warm, or you used a heat lamp, you know that you can't count on all of them hatching. Out of 12 eggs, you could have none, maybe five or six, and occasionally all 12! So claiming you are going to get 12 chicks from those 12 eggs is foolish. You count them once they hatch.

I'm a planner. I plan for everything, creating agendas and the next steps. I plan for the future. I plan for emergencies. I plan for possible events. I have even planned and paid for my funeral, even though I'm not rushing it!

The man in the parable was also a planner. He planned out his future. He was going to retire in luxury and comfort, and then party and entertain. Trouble was, he didn't consult

God about those plans. Neither did he include God in them, with the parable giving us no evidence of tithing or commitment to God in any way. That did not please God. The man dropped dead, and did not enjoy that luxurious retirement he had planned.

When I think about what this parable teaches me about God, I reach the conclusion that God doesn't want me to be self-reliant, trusting only in myself. He wants me to seek Him, consult Him, and trust Him.

My retirement plans have not gone exactly as I had planned either. I had realized that cancer could be a part of it and had purchased a cancer insurance policy. I was thinking that if I got cancer, it would be caught early, and I would get treatment, and move on with life. I never thought of an incurable leukemia, never dreamed I'd have something I would need to deal with for the remainder of my life.

But oh, how much have I learned! Yes, there are lessons about blood, bone marrow, lymph system, and parts of the body affected by the unhealthy blood cells. Those are good lessons, but not the important ones, which are all spiritual: Lean on God, not on my own understanding; Persevere; Trust in His next steps; Realize His agenda is better than mine; Accept that His timetable is perfect; Seek His help as I make plans.

The lessons learned are worth the journey. Maybe I'm also learning to "not count my chicks before they hatch."

Prayer: *Lord, help me to let go, to let You, to not rely on myself, but to consult You in each step I take. Help me realize that* *things that happen to me are for my own good. I will learn and grow through each one. Keep me from "counting my chicks before they hatch."*

Proverbs 3:5-6 Living Bible (TLB)
4-5 If you want favor with both God and man, and a reputation for good judgment and common sense, then trust the Lord completely; don't ever trust yourself. 6 In everything you do, put God first, and He will direct you and crown your efforts with success.

Romans 5:3-5 Modern English Version (MEV)
3 Not only so, but we also boast in tribulation, knowing that tribulation produces patience, 4 patience produces character, and character produces hope. 5 And hope does not disappoint, because the love of God is shed abroad in our hearts by the Holy Spirit who has been given to us.

DON'T JUDGE A BOOK BY ITS COVER

Matthew 7:1-5 The Voice (VOICE)
7 Jesus: If you judge other people, then you will find that you, too, are being judged. ² Indeed, you will be judged by the very standards to which you hold other people.

So when someone is tempted to criticize his neighbor because her house isn't clean enough, she seems ill-tempered, or she is a bit flighty—he should remember those same standards and judgments will come back to him. No one should criticize his neighbor for being short-tempered one morning, when he is snippish and snappish and waspish all the time.

Jesus: ³ Why is it that you see the dust in your brother's or sister's eye, but you can't see what is in your own eye? ⁴ Don't ignore the wooden plank in your eye, while you criticize the speck of sawdust in your brother's eyelashes. ⁵ That type of criticism and judgment is a sham! Remove the plank from your own eye, and then perhaps you will be able to see clearly how to help your brother flush out his sawdust.

It's so easy to be judgmental and so difficult to be full of grace and not criticize what we don't like. Yet Jesus says very clearly that the standards I hold other people to are the standards to which I'll be held. Ouch.

Years ago, I sat by a lady on a flight with whom I talked, and found I really liked her. She seemed so kind, so full of energy, so willing to help others. She was an author of romance novels, so I checked out her books online, and liked the look of them. I purchased one of her books to read. The book had a good story line, yet was the story of people with values very different from mine. There was no moral to the story. I found myself wondering what kind of lifestyle this wife, mom, and friendly lady really had. I was judging the lady, not the book, by the cover that she had presented.

Another time, I met a different author and looked at her books online. The covers made me know immediately that the values were not mine – I did "judge the book by the cover," and never bought one of her books.

I'm afraid I have done the same thing with people – judged them by their dress, their skin color, their language, their attitude. I'm not proud of it, but I've done it. I have even said things like, "Love the sinner, hate the sin." But I think Mark Lowry has a much better statement:

> "Love the sinner, hate the sin? How about: Love the sinner, hate your own sin! I don't have time to hate your sin. There are too many of you! Hating my sin is a full-time job. How about you hate your sin, I'll hate my sin and let's just love each other!"

Wow, wouldn't the world be better if we all did that! Hatred would be erased. Christians would not be judging other folks by the covers they have (new or old car, revealing clothing, or lifestyle choices, for example). Non-Christians would not assume (judge) that all Christians are judgmental. We could like and respect each other for who we are. Jesus warned us that we would be judged by the standards we judge others, so let's quit judging people by their covers.

***Prayer:** Lord, help me look at each person that I am with, old and new relationships, with the love that You showed when You lived on earth. Help me hate my own sin and love other sinners just as they are. It's Your job to do any judging that needs to be done. Help me let go of the judging habit. Grow me. Thank You.*

"No matter what you do, someone will have something negative to say. Try not to take it personally. People judge and criticize other people's lives when they're not happy with their own." Lori Deschene

Zechariah 7:9 - 10 AMP

Thus has the Lord of hosts spoken: Execute true judgment and show mercy and kindness and tender compassion, every man to his brother. And oppress not the widow or the fatherless, the temporary resident or the poor, and let none of you devise or imagine or think evil against his brother in your heart.

"Fear-based repentance makes us hate ourselves. Joy-based repentance makes us hate the sin." Tim Keller

EARLY TO BED, EARLY TO RISE, MAKES A MAN HEALTHY, WEALTHY, AND WISE

Proverbs 6:6 (NLT)
Take a lesson from the ants, you lazybones. Learn from their ways and become wise!

Matthew 25:24-27 International Children's Bible (ICB)
²⁴ "Then the servant who got one bag of money came to the master. The servant said, 'Master, I knew that you were a hard man. You harvest things you did not plant. You gather crops where you did not sow any seed. ²⁵ So I was afraid. I went and hid your money in the ground. Here is the bag of money you gave me.' ²⁶ The master answered, 'You are a bad and lazy servant! You say you knew that I harvest things I did not plant, and that I gather crops where I did not sow any seed? ²⁷ So you should have put my money in the bank. Then, when I came home, I would get my money back with interest.'

Growing up on a farm in the 1940s-1960s, I often heard the phrase, "Early to bed, early to rise, makes a man, healthy, and wealthy, and wise." My dad was up before sunrise to feed the animals, and mom was up by sunrise to start breakfast, milk the cow, and let the chickens out to free-roam. Dad would sometimes go to the fields to work for an hour or two before coming back for breakfast. Then he would work until noon, eat a big meal, and take a nap before returning to the fields to work until time for supper. At certain times of the year, there was much to be done after the evening meal until sunset. Shortly after sunset, he was in bed, sound asleep. If I wanted to stay in bed in the early morning, I was reminded, "Early to bed, early to rise, makes a man healthy, and wealthy and wise." So I developed a strong work ethic early in life, and have continued to be a hard worker for the most of it.

Is that what God wants of us? Yes, I think so, but I also need to remember that God himself took the seventh day off to rest, so rest needs to be a part of my life as well. Looking at the two scriptures above, I see that Solomon, who wrote most of the proverbs, suggests that we should not be lazy, and that we should learn from the ants, who are very hardworking little creatures, able to carry a load much heavier that their body weight. The parable that Jesus told about the men to whom were delegated some ways to invest at various values (five, two, and one) illustrates that the men who invested wisely were rewarded, whereas the one who did nothing was reprimanded for his poor decision, his laziness. These, combined with other verses in the Bible, tell me that God wants me to use resources wisely, and that often means "early to bed, early to rise" in order to reach the potential that we have to be "healthy, wealthy, and wise."

***Prayer:** Father God, who worked hard for six days, and then rested, help us to be good stewards of the resources You have provided for us, including time, energy, and money, that we* *may have adequate to be able to share generously with others, and to have security for ourselves. Help us find balance as we approach life, seeking health, wealth, and wisdom in daily life. Thank You.*

"The only place where success comes before work is in the dictionary."
Vidal Sassoon

"A dream does not become reality through magic; it takes sweat, determination, and hard work."
Colin Powell

"Satisfaction lies in the effort, not in attainment."
Mahatma Gandi

GET YOUR DUCKS ALL IN A ROW

1 Corinthians 14:40 (NIV)
But everything should be done in a fitting and orderly way.

Recently, I was down by the lake behind my condo building. I noticed a Mama Duck with eight little hatchlings, not more than a day or two old. She was letting them swim, but it was dusk, and they were soon tired and ready for their night's rest. Mama scrambled up the bank, and the ducklings were right behind her, finding it difficult to make it up the steep embankment. She approached the last one, helped it make those last steps, checked her brood, and started across the grass toward their likely place of shelter for the evening, some tall, thick cattails and vegetation. Each duckling quickly got in line behind her, and I of course thought of this idiom and the hundreds of times I've used it! When I do a presentation, or teach a class, I'm careful to have all my "ducks in a row" or I am not relaxed, and don't do as good a job. When I start to work on income tax, or any other big project, the same is true – I want my "ducks in a row." It boosts my confidence.

In I Corinthians 14:26-40, Paul talks about a worship time that was not orderly, and then instructs them to not be that way, but to have a plan, to be orderly in what they do. Now I don't think Paul was legalistic, and I don't think he was asking you to create some traditions and follow them the rest of your lives when you are together. Instead, I think he was saying that meeting together as Christians needs to be planned, organized, and perhaps even efficient. And isn't the same true in life? Isn't the principle applicable to other aspects of life? An orderly and organized life brings peace and contentment to most of us. Chaos is confusing, unsettling.

Think about the creation. What if God had created man before He created air, light, or plants and animals? Man would not have had air to breath, not been able to use the eyes God had given him, and would have had nothing to eat! Yes, there was an orderly plan to creation. It was not haphazard.

Jesus was also orderly. He had a plan. He waited 30 years before He called His apostles. Then He trained them before He sent them out to teach and preach. He prepared them for His death, His resurrection, His return. And He left an orderly plan for us - the Bible, which at first awareness may not seem orderly, but further study finds it very much so.

Yes, I like my "ducks in a row". Like those little hatchlings I was watching, they get out of line often, but with God's help, I'm able to get them back, and life is easier, adding to my contentment and peace.

Prayer: God of organization, chaos is so frustrating. Help me to be orderly in my approach to my various activities and help me keep from wandering off the path. You had "Your ducks in a row." I want You to be my example, and I want to follow in Your footsteps. That means I need to have my "ducks in a row."

"By failing to prepare, you are preparing to fail."
Benjamin Franklin

<u>Jeremiah 29:11 NIV</u>

For I know the plans I have for you," declares the Lord, "plans to prosper you and not to harm you, plans to give you hope and a future.

STUFFING TEN POUNDS OF POTATOES INTO A FIVE POUND BAG

Hebrews 12:1-2 Amplified Bible, Classic Edition (AMPC)
Therefore then, since we are surrounded by so great a cloud of witnesses [who have borne testimony to the Truth], let us strip off and throw aside every encumbrance (unnecessary weight) and that sin which so readily (deftly and cleverly) clings to and entangles us, and let us run with patient endurance and steady and active persistence the appointed course of the race that is set before us.

Psalm 46:10 Amplified Bible, Classic Edition (AMPC)
[10] Let be and be still, and know (recognize and understand) that I am God. I will be exalted among the nations! I will be exalted in the earth!

Do you know the story of Mary and Martha (Luke 10:38-42)? Martha was "busy as a bee," trying to get a big dinner ready because a special guest was visiting her home. In modern day America, she would have wanted fresh flowers on the table, the best wine, fresh bread that made the house smell wonderful, with good herbed butter. The leg of lamb would need to be just perfect, and the vegetables would have been fresh from the garden, with rich and delectable sauces for their enhancement. Lentil soup was likely cooking on the back burner, and honey cakes were baking in the oven so there would be tasty dessert.

Mary sat quietly at the feet of Jesus, soaking in every word He said, wanting to know how to better live so she could be kind and compassionate like Jesus, more godly. Martha had a "bee in her bonnet," and was not at all happy that her little sister Mary was not helping with all the preparations. She felt like she was "stuffing ten pounds of potatoes into a five-pound sack." She felt miserable, and she let it be known. Jesus's response was simple: "Mary has chosen the better. Be still. I'd be content with stale bread and milk."

For years, I took pride in being over-busy. I loved being busy, doing things for others, doing my job well, taking on projects, and executing them in creative and exciting ways. Then I heard an interview of Dallas Willard on talk radio, and he said "You need to ruthlessly eliminate hurry from your life." What? My life had been one of hurry for fifty years. Change my habits, my ways? I couldn't get that thought out of my mind, and it kept nagging at me. Eventually, I resolved to slow down and do less, which has led to reduced stress, and has helped me adapt to isolation during the pandemic we are experiencing as I write these devotionals. I no longer have any desire to "stuff ten pounds of potatoes into a five-pound bag." I like having time to "be still, to know God." I found that being busy tends to be an unneeded weight. Ridding myself of it has led to feeling that the course I am on is more aligned with how my life should be, to more peace, to greater spiritual blessings – and I'll take them over material blessings, any day!

A study of these and other verses shows us clearly that God prefers us to have a balanced life, including the things that make us comfortable and provide our daily physical and material needs, but also that provides for our spiritual needs. That is the true comfort zone.

Prayer: Life can be so busy. People have so many needs, and some of us have so many ideas that we enjoy executing. Bosses will call on us to do more and more if we accept the challenge. We can volunteer and use up every spare moment of our time. Help each of us to find balance in our lives, to do the things we need to do, and yet to choose to balance those things by having time with You, so You can fill the spiritual well within each of us. Thank You, God who is content with bread and milk.

"A plan is what, a schedule is when. It takes both a plan and a schedule to get things done." Peter Turla

"Take a rest. A field that has rested yields a beautiful crop." Ovid

Ecclesiastes 3:1-8 New International Version (NIV)

3 There is a time for everything,
and a season for every activity under the heavens:
²a time to be born and a time to die,
a time to plant and a time to uproot,
³a time to kill and a time to heal,
a time to tear down and a time to build,
⁴a time to weep and a time to laugh,
a time to mourn and a time to dance,
⁵a time to scatter stones and a time to gather them,
a time to embrace and a time to refrain from embracing,

[6] a time to search and a time to give up,
a time to keep and a time to throw away,
[7] a time to tear and a time to mend,
a time to be silent and a time to speak,
[8] a time to love and a time to hate,
a time for war and a time for peace.

FOOTLOOSE AND FANCY FREE

Luke 15:11-14 World English Bible (WEB)
¹¹ He said, "A certain man had two sons. ¹² The younger of them said to his father, 'Father, give me my share of your property.' So he divided his livelihood between them. ¹³ Not many days after, the younger son gathered all of this together and traveled into a far country. There he wasted his property with riotous living. ¹⁴ When he had spent all of it, there arose a severe famine in that country, and he began to be in need.

We call him "The Prodigal Son." Why? Because he took the money his dad gave him, ran off, and lived "footloose and fancy free." It seemed fun at first – using that money to buy a round of drinks for everyone, buying girlfriends nice gifts, spending on himself for anything he wanted. Only trouble was that when the money ran out, so did the "friends." He was alone, hungry, and homeless, so he did the only thing he knew to do – get a job. Jobs weren't readily available for him, however, so he took a job tending pigs, a job any respectable Jewish boy would avoid at all costs. But he was no longer a respectable Jewish boy – he was a desperate Jewish boy in an unfamiliar culture.

We all desire freedom. We want to be able to do what we want to do and when we want to do it. We start telling our parents "No!" when we are toddlers, and we keep challenging the boundaries throughout life. Teen years are a time when we often test the "footloose and fancy free" lifestyle, challenging the limits we've accepted in childhood. This may even lead to rebellion. Hopefully, we learn from the experience that boundaries are there for our own good, and that wisdom suggests that we set our own boundaries in life.

If we read further in this scripture, we learn that this boy "came to his senses." He surrendered his will and began to eat from his father's bounty – in fact, his dad even threw a party for him. That's what God wants all of us to do. Think of God as the father in this story, and realize that Jesus is telling us the story so we can recognize that God's arms are open wide as He waits and watches for us to come home.

Prayer: Lord, I surrender my stubborn desire to be "footloose and fancy free" to You, who created and designed me. I anxiously await the joy of sitting at the table with You to enjoy Your presence, to be assured of Your love in spite of my past. You love me just as I am. Thank You that Your arms are open, You are waiting and watching, wanting me to run to You. I feel like a toddler running toward unconditional love.

"You are free to make whatever choice you want, but you are not free from the consequences of the choice."
Anonymous

"May your choices reflect your hopes, not your fears."
Nelson Mandela

GIVE IT A LICK AND A PROMISE

Exodus 34:21 NIV
²¹ "Six days you shall labor, but on the seventh day you shall rest; even during the plowing season and harvest you must rest.

Exodus 35:10 NIV
¹⁰ "All who are skilled among you are to come and make everything the Lord has commanded:

Exodus 39:43 NIV
⁴³ Moses inspected the work and saw that they had done it just as the Lord had commanded. So Moses blessed them.

Colossians 3:24 Easy-to-Read Version (ERV)
²⁴ Remember that you will receive your reward from the Lord, who will give you what He promised His people. Yes, you are serving Christ. He is your Master.[a]

Have you ever read the book of Exodus, the second book of the Bible? If not, I encourage you to do so. Likely you've seen a movie about Moses, so even if you've never read the book, you know some parts of the story.

One of the ten commandments that God gave the Jewish people was to rest. He gave them a day of the week that they were to rest. When you read the remainder of the Exodus, you can see why they needed to rest! They worked hard.

God gave them some specific instructions to build a tabernacle, so they collected up the resources needed for it - fine woods, fibers, gold, silver, jewels, etc. The people gave so much that Moses had to ask them not to give any more. Then the skilled craftsmen and women went to work, doing everything as their blueprint had laid out. The part of the world where they lived was hot and dry much of the year. There was no AC in which to work. But they worked, and finally got the tabernacle completed. That's when Moses inspected the work, and found that it had been done with excellence, just as they had been instructed. So he blessed the workers.

When I think of buildings constructed today, I think of some that are not built "just as instructed." Some contractors like to use shortcuts, do things to save a few dollars here, there and yon, "give it a lick and a promise." As a result, the building often has issues – perhaps rain blows in around a window, the floor is not level, the carpet isn't stretched properly, and the list goes on and on. Those workmen are not blessed by the new owner of the building, and that company likely won't get the next contract they issue.

Why should you do your work with excellence? Paul tells us that we are to work to please God, and that we will receive a reward for doing a job well. We know from experience that work well done is usually rewarded here on earth, too. I feel better when I can look back on a job with pride, knowing it was done properly. Yet, most of us have times when we don't – we are in a hurry, or perhaps don't have the skill, or we're fatigued, a common problem for those of us with cancer and for people with many other diseases. But I don't want to eat off dishes that are not washed properly, or drive on roads not paved correctly and have too many potholes! It's a rare task where excellence doesn't matter. That's why I've asked several people to proofread these devotionals, but knowing full well it likely will still have mistakes when it goes to print! (Sorry, but we are trying!)

Yes, God likes work done with excellence. He did His work with excellence, and then He rested. May you and I do the same.

Prayer: *Thank You Lord for the skills You have given us to do our work with excellence, and to recognize when we've done a job well. Thank You for rewarding us for good work. Help us to purpose to do our work to honor You, to have the right attitude as we work, and to avoid doing important things "with a lick and a promise." Your work was excellent, and we applaud You, and want to be more like You.*

"Shortcuts make long delays." J.R.R. Tolkien

"I can because God can and He lives in me." David Platt

"Do or do not. There is no **try**." Yoda

HE SQUEALED LIKE A PIG UNDER THE GATE

Ecclesiastes 7:21-22 The Message (MSG)
²¹⁻²² Don't eavesdrop on the conversation of others. What if the gossip's about you and you'd rather not hear it? You've done that a few times, haven't you—said things Behind someone's back you wouldn't say to his face?

Ephesians 4:29-30 The Message (MSG)
²⁹ Watch the way you talk. Let nothing foul or dirty come out of your mouth. Say only what helps, each word a gift.

³⁰ Don't grieve God. Don't break His heart. His Holy Spirit, moving and breathing in you, is the most intimate part of your life, making you fit for Himself. Don't take such a gift for granted.

If you've ever been around pigs, you know they can squeal, especially even if in minor pain. And they get themselves in all kinds of predicaments because they want to break all the rules, ignore the boundaries of fences, because the grass seems greener on the other side. Basically, they just don't mind their own business. So they try to squeeze through small spaces. That's when they get stuck, and squeal.

I've noticed over the years that when I don't mind my own business, it usually leads me to gossip. Doing a search in the Bible about gossip, slander, or lying will lead you to the conclusion that God doesn't like them!

We've all been busybodies and all gossiped, even though we played the gossip game as a child and know full well that misinformation gets passed rapidly and inaccurately from one person to another. But it made us feel better for the moment. We subconsciously compare ourselves to that person, and think we look pretty good.

But if the gossip is about me – or you – I (or you) often "squeal like pig under the gate." We are in emotional pain. We don't like it when others talk about us, and the information gets mismanaged. But neither does God. He tells us plainly that we are to use words as gifts. Gossip is not a gift. Words behind another person's back are not gifts. They are stabs in the back.

Has God ever gossiped about you? I didn't think so. He was honest about the flaws of the people in the Bible. But gossip isn't honest (okay, maybe partially honest) and is not for anyone's good. The stories in the Bible all have value, have a purpose that is for good, often showing that God uses flawed people.

So what's the take-away lesson? Don't squeal on others, unless you want them to squeal on you. And since you don't, that means just don't do it.

> **Prayer:** *Lord, help me to be honest, but only to share what is wise. If others gossip about me, help me confront the issue and*

deal with it appropriately, even if I'm hurting. Forgive me for the times I've gossiped and thus put others into a bad situation. Keep me from squealing about people, and about the pain they inflict via their words on me.

"Gossiping and lying go hand in hand." Proverb

"Watch out for the joy-stealers: gossip, criticism, complaining, faultfinding, and a negative, judgmental attitude." Joyce Meyer

"People gossip. People are insecure, so they talk about other people so they won't be talked about. They point out flaws in other people to make them feel good about themselves." Blake Lively

1 Timothy 5:13 Easy-to-Read Version

[13] Also, these younger widows begin to waste their time going from house to house. They also begin to gossip and try to run other people's lives. They say things they should not say.

Ephesians 4:29 Disciples' Literal New Testament

[29] Let every bad word not proceed out of your mouth, but if *there is* something good for edification *of* the need, *speak* in order that it may give grace *to* the *ones* hearing

HAD TO EAT HUMBLE PIE

Daniel 4:32-33 New International Version (NIV)
³² You will be driven away from people and will live with the wild animals; you will eat grass like the ox. Seven times will pass by for you until you acknowledge that the Most High is sovereign over all kingdoms on earth and gives them to anyone He wishes."

³³ Immediately what had been said about Nebuchadnezzar was fulfilled. He was driven away from people and ate grass like the ox. His body was drenched with the dew of heaven until his hair grew like the feathers of an eagle and his nails like the claws of a bird.

John 1:14 Tree of Life Version (TLV)
¹⁴ And the Word became flesh and tabernacled among us. We looked upon His glory, the glory of the one and only[b] from the Father, full of grace and truth.

Humble pie, sometimes referred to as eating crow, does not taste good. I know from experience. Likely, you've tried it a few times too.

Compare Nebuchadnezzar to Jesus. King Neb was a proud man, determined to have the glory and honor that he thought he deserved. God even warned him that he'd be eating grass if he didn't get his act together, but he ignored the warning. A year later, he stood on the roof of his palace and bragged about all he had accomplished. He praised himself and ignored the role of God in his life. So he ate grass for seven years, and lived liked an animal.

Jesus, on the other hand, lived in heaven with His father God. Instead of exalting Himself and bragging, He entered the womb of a teenage girl, went through the birth canal, and lived 33 years in a rugged countryside, likely struggling to find much to eat, even grass! His life was hard, by His own choice. Times were hard, with the Roman government treating the Jewish people very poorly, and the Jewish leaders extorting their own people, making life even more difficult. His life got more difficult as He matured, ending in a very cruel death.

James 4:10 tells us to "humble ourselves before the Lord, and He will lift us up." I'm still learning that it's a lot easier to humble myself, than to let God do the humbling. When He does it, I'm ashamed, embarrassed, and don't want to show my face. When I surrender to Him, and humble myself, He elevates me, and I feel good, at peace. Try it, you might like it better than humble pie.

God keeps His word, so when He says He will exalt me, that's what He will do. He's proven himself true to me hundreds of times, and I trust Him to keep His word with this promise!

Prayer: Lord, I make mistakes. I need to humble myself when I do, admit it, and not try to hide it, as is my nature. Give me the courage to do so – I much prefer Your way to humble pie. Eating grass would be as bad as eating crow, and I'd rather just humble myself and surrender to Your way. You are not nearly as harsh as the natural consequences.

"Never look down on anyone unless you're helping them up." Jessie Jackson

"Humility is not thinking less of yourself, it's thinking of yourself less." C.S. Lewis

"'Thank you' is the best prayer that anyone could say. I say that one a lot. Thank you expresses extreme gratitude, humility, understanding." Alice Walker

I Peter 5:6 NIV

Humble yourselves, therefore, under God's might hand, that He may lift you up in due time.

IF YOU HOOT WITH THE OWLS, YOU CAN'T SOAR WITH THE EAGLES

Proverbs 14:8 The Voice (VOICE)

⁸ *It takes wisdom for the clever to understand the path they are on, but the fool is deceived by his own foolishness.*

Owls and eagles are among my favorite birds. Owls fascinate me with their ability to rotate their heads by almost 180 degrees. They can silently sail through the night air, and life below can be totally unaware of them. Eagles are more majestic, soaring on air currents far above the earth, with keen eyesight that can see a mile below, and the ability to time their landing on a fish or other prey with perfection. Both have great purpose in keeping wildlife balanced in our world, and both have a beauty unique to them.

I've been guilty of trying to be an owl, staying up too late, watching a football game, or doing something that seemed more interesting and fun than going to bed! The next day, I was exhausted, not able to perform my best, unable to soar above the challenges of the day without frustrations and with poor vision. I was trying to both "hoot with the owls and soar with the eagles," but I failed. As Solomon, the author of most of the Proverbs, says, my own foolishness deceived me.

I was married to a night owl. He had a very difficult time getting up in the morning, likely because he was so tired and sleepy from staying up so late. Obsessive compulsive ways seemed to rule his use of time, especially at night. He then wanted to sleep all day, which does not align with the world around us unless you have a nighttime job! Like me, he allowed his own foolishness to deceive him. Soaring with the eagles was impossible for him, because he didn't have the energy after sailing on the night currents with the owls.

The proverbs of the Bible are just that – proverbs or wise sayings. They are not promises. But all 31 chapters of the book of Proverbs have a lot of wisdom in them. Periodically, I like to read a chapter a day for a month, just to remind me of the lessons I've learned over the years, and some that I need to relearn. I believe that the sharing of the proverbs is a good way for God to show us that He really does want what is best for us, but also to remind us that He has given us our own will, and we can choose to use wisdom or choose to be foolish. Whichever we choose, we will reap the roses of wisdom or gather the thorns of foolishness.

Prayer: *Lord, help me to be willing to look to You for the wisdom I need, so that I don't try to both "hoot with the owls and soar with the eagles". Help me have the self-control that I need to not deceive myself with foolishness.*

"The invariable mark of wisdom is to see the miraculous in the common." Ralph Waldo Emerson

"Wisdom is the daughter of experience." Anonymous

"Wisdom is knowledge that is guided by understanding; we have to have the wisdom and the knowledge to understand why certain things happen in our lives and trust that God will lead us over any obstacle that comes in our way." Anonymous

"A wise owl sat on an oak, the more he saw the less he spoke, the less he spoke the more he heard. Why aren't we like the wise old bird?" Charles M. Schulz

KEEP A CIVIL TONGUE IN YOUR HEAD

Romans 13:10 Complete Jewish Bible (CJB)
¹⁰ Love does not do harm to a neighbor; therefore love is the fullness of Torah.

Deuteronomy 6:4-9 Holman Christian Standard Bible (HCSB)
⁴ Listen, Israel: The Lord our God, the Lord is One. ⁵ Love the Lord your God with all your heart, with all your soul, and with all your strength. ⁶ These words that I am giving you today are to be in your heart. ⁷ Repeat them to your children. Talk about them when you sit in your house and when you walk along the road, when you lie down and when you get up. ⁸ Bind them as a sign on your hand and let them be a symbol on your forehead.[c] ⁹ Write them on the doorposts of your house and on your gates.

Matthew 22:36-39 International Children's Bible (ICB)
³⁶ The Pharisee asked, "Teacher, which command in the law is the most important?"

³⁷ Jesus answered, "'Love the Lord your God with all your heart, soul and mind.' ³⁸ This is the first and most important command. ³⁹ And the second command is like the first: 'Love your neighbor as you love yourself.'"

Suggested Reading: Luke 10:25-37

Both the Old and New Testaments agree: Love God, and love your neighbor. Paul even says that love is what fulfills the law.

Chances are, even if you have never attended church, you know the phrase "good Samaritan" and know a little about the story in the suggested reading of Luke 10:25-37. An attorney asked Jesus what he needed to do to inherit eternal life. Jesus answered that he was to love God and love his neighbor. So he asked who his neighbor was, and Jesus told the story of religious leaders who ignored the needs of a man who had been beaten, robbed, and left to die. The conclusion is simple: The person who needs mercy is our neighbor. Close proximity in housing has nothing to do with it, nor does skin tone, ethnicity, religion, etc. Bottom line is that we are to be merciful to all people and we will be good neighbors.

Me: But wait a minute, Lord. I'm not comfortable with *that person*. He's different. She's obnoxious. His political ideas are not the same as mine. Her social media presence makes me feel uncomfortable. He doesn't even believe You exist! And she constantly curses You, doesn't have a civil tongue in her mouth.

Jesus: Be merciful. Show love. Look and act like me. You are the one I call to have a civil tongue. You are not responsible for what others do, only what you do. So keep your tongue (and your social media postings, and all your communications) civil. I'll help you, by my Holy Spirit.

That's what makes a good neighbor. Love me, and you will love your neighbor.

Me: But that's not easy!

Jesus: No, it's not. Important stuff is not easy. Learning to tie your shoes was not easy. Learning to add and subtract took work. Being a parent is hard work, it's lots of effort. Just remember, like my brother James said, "The tongue is a small part of the body, but it makes great boasts... The tongue is a fire, a world of evil among the parts of the body." So keep it civil, and sometimes that means the cat needs to hold your tongue so that you say nothing!

Me: Yes, Lord.

Prayer: Oh, Lord, it is so hard to keep a civil tongue! I'm so glad You gave me a helper, Your Holy Spirit, to empower me and to use my tongue to create a better neighbor to all kinds of folks, even those I don't particularly like. You love them, and that's reason enough for me to treat them with mercy and kindness. Thank You for helping me because I cannot do it on my own.

James 3:5-12 The Voice (VOICE)

[5] It's just the same with our tongues! It's a small muscle, capable of marvelous undertakings. And do you know how many forest fires begin with a single ember from a small campfire? [6] The tongue is a blazing fire seeking to ignite an entire world of vices. The tongue is unique among all parts of the body because it is capable of corrupting the whole body. If that were not enough, it ignites and consumes the course of creation with a fuel

that originates in hell itself. ⁷ Humanity is capable of taming every bird and beast in existence, even reptiles and sea creatures great and small. ⁸ But no man has ever demonstrated the ability to tame his own tongue! It is a spring of restless evil, brimming with toxic poisons. ⁹ Ironically this same tongue can be both an instrument of blessing to our Lord and Father and a weapon that hurls curses upon others who are created in God's own image. ¹⁰ One mouth streams forth both blessings and curses. My brothers and sisters, this is not how it should be. ¹¹ Does a spring gush crystal clear freshwater and moments later spurt out bitter salt water? ¹² My brothers and sisters, does a fig tree produce olives? Is there a grapevine capable of growing figs? Can saltwater give way to freshwater?

WHEN LIFE GIVES YOU LEMONS, MAKE LEMONADE

John 18:27 The Passion Translation (TPT)
²⁷ Then Peter denied it the third time and said, "No!"—and at that very same moment, a rooster crowed nearby.

1 Peter 1:6 The Passion Translation (TPT)
⁶ May the thought of this cause you to jump for joy, even though lately you've had to put up with the grief of many trials.

As I contemplate this colloquial statement, I think of so many Biblical characters who did this – they allowed very bad and sour circumstances to shape them into better people, and they grew in the fruit of the Spirit. Consider Job. Meditate on the life of Joseph. How would you like to live in caves as David often did? John grew old as his fellow apostles were killed off one by one, and look what a treasury he left us as a result of the trials in his life! The list goes on and on.

But let's consider Peter. Liar. Impetuous. People pleaser. Like a lot of us. Snapshots of his lifestyle make us wonder why Jesus chose him as an apostle, and certainly why He would choose him to give that sermon in Acts 2! Oh, he was not a drug addict, or a thief, or a murderer. He was just an ordinary man stumbling through life, trying to look good, "be somebody," or perhaps make a name for himself.

But I'm so glad Jesus used him, because if He can use Peter, He can use me (and you). I stumble, too. I make some pretty bad decisions, trying to look good, trying to be what people want me to be. I can be very foolish, blaming others rather than taking responsibility. And when Jesus turns around and looks at me, I want to crawl off in shame. I imagine Peter was totally embarrassed when that rooster crowed. Been there, done that, got that tee shirt. You too? That's when it's time to have a "come to Jesus" moment, just like Peter did. Then, we can make lemonade - lemonade that gets sweeter over time, as we develop and mature in Jesus, becoming more loving, gentle, patient, persevering, and self-controlled.

***Prayer:** Lord of lemons, help me make lemonade every time I mess up. Work on my attitude and show me how to look at circumstances that are not pleasant, perhaps even embarrassing, and turn them into sweetness that reflects You and Your nature. My trust and faith are in You.*

"No man is broken because bad things happen to him. He's broken because he doesn't keep going after those things happen." Courtney Milan in Unraveled

"The good and the bad things are part of life. Accept it. The bad is a learning process, you will surpass it. If you do you will be happy and it will be a good thing."
Ann Marie Aguilar

"I figure, sometimes, bad things happen to us so we can achieve a higher purpose and attain a greater happiness and fulfillment in life." Omoakhuana Anthonia

IF THE SHOE FITS, WEAR IT

Proverbs 15:22 International Children's Bible (ICB)
²² Plans fail without good advice.
But plans succeed when you get advice from many others.

Luke 8:16-18 J.B. Phillips New Testament (PHILLIPS)
¹⁶⁻¹⁷ Nobody lights a lamp and covers it with a basin or puts it under the bed. No, a man puts his lamp on a lamp-stand so that those who come in can see the light. For there is nothing hidden now which will not become perfectly plain and there are no secrets now which will not become as clear as daylight.

¹⁸ So take care how you listen—more will be given to the man who has something already, but the man who has nothing will lose even what he thinks he has.

Shoes: they fit, or they don't. There is no in-between. For those of us with slim feet, most often they don't! As a result, I've had blisters, bunions, planter fasciitis, and all kinds of foot problems. So when I do find a pair of shoes that truly fits, I buy them in at least a couple of colors, and keep trying that name-brand in hopes that their next styles will fit, too.

Lessons of life: events, circumstances, and the people in your life fit, or they don't. But if it's something you need to learn, claim it, don't deny it. Accept that the lesson is meant for you and make it a part of your life, just as I make those shoes a part of my life.

Need an example? I love to walk, particularly out in nature. Parks, woods, dirt roads – I can walk them for hours, enjoying the scenery, watching the butterflies, bees, birds, wildlife, looking at plants, etc. But the last few years, I've coped with low sodium. Walking outside in Florida in high humidity makes me sweat. I lose sodium via that perspiration. Then I don't feel good, lose energy, get confused. So it's foolish for me to walk outside in the heat of the summer. The shoe fits, so I'd best wear it, or I will pay the consequences. So I heed my doctor's advice and walk inside on a treadmill most of the hot months of the year. I'm enlightened, so I don't ignore the real-life situation that I have. The light has revealed my problem. Denying it just puts me in darkness, and gives me issues.

I recall a friend many years ago who had diabetes. She would often say, "Just one little bite of that pie won't hurt me." Once she started, she ate an entire piece, maybe two. Those little bites led to her early death. She had the light, but she chose the darkness of denial. She suffered for hundreds of hours because of her denial.

Does God deny things? I don't think so. I think He sees the world as it is. He sees our hearts, and He works with us to shed light on our issues. It's up to us to "wear the shoes that fit."

> ***Prayer***: *Lord, it's so much easier to keep doing things I've always done, even things that are foolish. Shed the light on*

those bad habits I have, on health issues, on relationship issues, on my foolish ways, so that I may see clearly and wear shoes that fit me, rather than shoes that will create blisters, bunions, and difficulty walking the good life. Thank you.

"When denial is in play, a person simply refuses to recognize the truth, no matter how apparent."
Taite Adams

"Denial exists when three beliefs intersect: 1. It cannot happen. 2. It cannot happen to you. 3. It cannot happen to you now." Johnnie Dent, Jr.

"God's delay is not God's denial." Robert H. Schuller

EVERY CLOUD HAS A SILVER LINING

Romans 8:28 1599 Geneva Bible (GNV)
²⁸ Also we know that all things work together for the best unto them that love God, even to them that are called of His purpose.

Romans 8:26-28 The Message (MSG)
²⁶⁻²⁸ Meanwhile, the moment we get tired in the waiting, God's Spirit is right alongside helping us along. If we don't know how or what to pray, it doesn't matter. He does our praying in and for us, making prayer out of our wordless sighs, our aching groans. He knows us far better than we know ourselves, knows our pregnant condition, and keeps us present before God. That's why we can be so sure that every detail in our lives of love for God is worked into something good.

I've heard my mom say "Every cloud has a silver lining" many times. Later in life, Thomas the Train and friends made the phrase popular with preschool children, as they sang "Life has ups and downs" and "every cloud a silver lining even when it rains."

The language of the verses above is quite different, with one from the centuries old 1599 translation of the Bible from the original language, and the second a paraphrase from modern times. Yet, the message is the same. There will be good to come out of the bad things happening in our lives. There's no promise of when. In fact, when God had Jeremiah talk to the Jewish people (Jeremiah 29:10-14), He told them that good things would be happening for the Jewish nation, but He didn't tell them it would be 400 years later! In our lives, it may be years down the road before we can look back and see that a difficult time had a silver lining, and that a lot of good came from it. But we can be assured that the time will come, and that a lot of good will come our way in God's perfect timing. He knows what is best for us, and while most bad things that happen to us are either the results of our own failure to consistently make wise decisions (choosing too much of the wrong foods, poor exercise or rest habits, failure to prepare for an exam, etc.), or perhaps another person's poor judgment (automobile accidents, abuse, addictions, for example), He can still take the situations and turn them into good lessons and experiences that prepare us for the next phases of our lives. Sometimes, even our family members learn from our mistakes.

So the next time you start to complain, look instead for the silver lining. Think back to things that have happened in the past and remind yourself of the silver linings that you've had. These verses teach us, in modern terms, that God has our back, and will make good out of whatever comes our way. Think about the lyrics to "Every Cloud Has a Silver Lining" that most preschoolers know well, having watched Bob, Ben, and of course, Thomas the Train!

Prayer: *Dear God of silver linings, who can take bad and turn it into good, teach me through the trials of life to look for the good in whatever comes my way, not to be quick to complain, but instead to be quick to believe that good will be coming my way. Thank You for making silver linings in the clouds that form in our lives.*

KILL 'EM WITH KINDNESS

> *Romans 12:20-21 New Testament for Everyone (NTE)*
> [20] *If your enemy is hungry, feed him; if he is thirsty, give him a drink. If you do this, you will pile up burning coals on his head.'*
> [21] *Don't let evil conquer you. Rather, conquer evil with good.*

> *Matthew 5:38-42 Easy-to-Read Version (ERV)*
> [38] *You have heard that it was said, 'An eye for an eye, and a tooth for a tooth.'* [39] *But I tell you, don't fight back against someone who wants to do harm to you. If they hit you on the right cheek, let them hit the other cheek too.* [40] *If anyone wants to sue you in court and take your shirt, let them have your coat too.* [41] *If a soldier forces you to walk with him one mile,[b] go with him two.* [42] *Give to anyone who asks you for something. Don't refuse to give to anyone who wants to borrow from you.*

As a child, I got my feelings hurt easily. To make it worse, I was a tattletale and complained about how people treated me. Children haven't changed – they still do the same thing! I heard about those hurt feelings as a teacher and principal. If you've been around children, you too have heard them – and like me, it's likely you did them.

My response, at least in my mind, was often the same as the response given to me: "Kill 'em with kindness!" I may not have said those exact words, but I tried to teach the principle. I often used the "golden rule" to help them understand. Paul and Matthew tell us in the verses above to do good for those who we feel have harmed us. Help them. Maybe pray for God to bless them as He sees fit. What happens then? They feel like they have burning coals on their heads! Ouch!

Yet, even if they are slow to come around to treating us as they should, Paul still admonishes us to not allow their evil to conquer us. We would then be "stooping to their level." Instead, we are to simply keep doing good, although there are times that Jesus shows us we need to follow His example and set some healthy boundaries so they are not abusing us. That actually may be the way we can show love the most.

But is it easy? No way! Our nature is to want to get even, to give them a tongue lashing, to repay evil with evil. It takes commitment and hard work to do otherwise. Healthier relationships come forth as a result, and we develop new friends in the process (with the exception of those times it is true abuse – those take intervention most of the time).

I recall a time when the relationship I had with a Christian brother was strained, and I felt that his way of dealing with an issue was totally inappropriate. I began to pray for God to bless him as God saw fit. Because God changed us both for the better, I can now ask for his help with any project without reservation. We each have great things to say about the other. It was not comfortable to begin those prayers. A tongue lashing would have been easy for me to give. I'm thankful that I made the hard choice and did what was best and right.

Prayer: *Lord, help me as I go through life. Relationships are hard. You know because You created us and then lived as one of us. Help me to bless, not curse, to "kill 'em with kindness." It will be worth it, because You are in charge of any revenge that is needed. I am weak. You are strong.*

"Vengeance, retaliation, retribution, revenge are deceitful brothers – vile, beguiling demons promising justifiable compensation to a pained soul for his losses. Yet in truth they craftily fester away all else of worth remaining."
Richelle E. Goodrich

"Just keep loving them. And by the power of your love they will break down under the load. That's love, you see. It is redemptive and this is why Jesus says love. There's something about love that builds up and it's creative. There is something about hate that tears down and is destructive. So love your enemies." Martin Luther King

"He promised there will never be a dark night that does not end. And by dying for us, Jesus showed how far our love should be ready to go – all the way." Ronald Reagan

MAKE HAY WHILE THE SUN SHINES

Colossians 3:23-24 (NIV)
²³Whatever you do, work at it with all your heart, as working for the Lord, not for human masters, since you know that you will receive an inheritance from the Lord as a reward. It is the Lord Christ you are serving.

Farmers are up early. They value sunshine and rain and know what needs to be done during any type of weather. There are some jobs that must be done when the sun is shining, not when it's raining. For example, the hay must be baled and prepared for the animals to enjoy when there is no green grass for them to eat. Thus the saying, "Make hay while the sun shines."

Rainy days are also valued by the farmers for they bring much needed moisture to the plants and animals. Those are not wasted days. The chickens still need to be fed, the cows need to be milked, and the garden needs to be tended between rain showers. Repairs can be made inside the barns or the house. Newborn animals need to be checked, no matter what the weather is. Rest is also valuable to the farmers, so a rainy day may provide time for an extended nap to refresh the soul and body.

HOMESPUN DEVOTION

Most farmers also are "working for the Lord." Go to a Farm Bureau meeting, and you will find prayers being said before every meal and function. These hard-working men and women know that farming depends on God, because the rain, sunshine, soil, and so many other things are in His control. They trust and rely on Him.

As a Christian, the "Son" is always shining in my life. But the sun is sometimes behind the clouds that envelope me. It's easier for me to "make hay" when the sun is brightly shining, yet there are jobs that need to be done whether or not the sun is shining on my life. Both the rain and sunshine of life are needed for the fruit of the spirit (love, joy, peace, patience, kindness, goodness, faithfulness, gentleness, and self-control) to develop in my life, just as the apple tree or bean stalk need rain and sunshine to develop their fruit. Life's trials may draw me to my knees in prayer and submission. That, likely, will be one of the times when I grow and mature the most. It's in those times that my "work" most glorifies God.

Without the rain, there would be no grass to mow for the hay. Without the sunshine, the cut grass would mold and rot. Life is the same. We need the rainy days of life to grow and develop. We need the sunshine to prepare for the future.

> ***Prayer:*** *God of the weather, who brings the sunshine and the rain to the earth, and who allows good and trying times in my life, help me have the right attitude no matter what storm of life I face. Help me "make hay while the sun shines" and use the rain to nourish my soul.*

"Never leave till tomorrow that which you can do today." Benjamin Franklin

"For the Present is the point at which time touches eternity." C.S. Lewis

"Take care of the minutes and the hours will take care of themselves." Lord Chesterfield

MESSY AS A SOUP SANDWICH

Genesis 37:31-35 New International Reader's Version (NIRV)
31 Then they got Joseph's beautiful robe. They killed a goat and dipped the robe in the blood. 32 They took the robe back to their father. They said, "We found this. Take a look at it. See if it's your son's robe."

33 Jacob recognized it. He said, "It's my son's robe! A wild animal has eaten him up. Joseph must have been torn to pieces."

34 Jacob tore his clothes. He put on the rough clothing people wear when they're sad. Then he mourned for his son many days. 35 All Jacob's other sons and daughters came to comfort him. But they weren't able to. He said, "I will continue to mourn until I go down into the grave to be with my son." So Joseph's father mourned for him.

Exodus 34:6-7 Easy-to-Read Version (ERV)
6 That is, the Lord passed in front of Moses and said, "Yahweh, the Lord, is a kind and merciful God. He is slow to become angry. He is full of great love. He can be trusted. 7 He shows His faithful love to thousands of people. He forgives people for the wrong things they do, but He does not forget to punish guilty people. Not only will He punish the guilty people, but their

children, their grandchildren, and their great-grandchildren will also suffer for the bad things these people do."

Joseph's family was messy, like a soup sandwich. His brothers were jealous to the extent that most were willing to kill their younger brother. All were willing to lie and deceive. Yet it is a beautiful story of forgiveness and redemption, and one from which we can learn a lot.

Imagine how they must have felt when their father needed sympathy, empathy, and reassurance from his family. Did they stuff their feelings in denial? Did they feel regret? Did they ever consider fessing up? Because we know how the story ends, we see a story of redemption, but consider the weight they carried in their hearts for all those years. Did that make the family even messier? Probably. Their children likely had families just as messy, and then those children passed it on to the next generation just as God told Moses would happen to families in Exodus 34:6-7.

God is a forgiving God. He loves us. Yet He is just, and He will punish us if we don't turn from our severely dysfunctional ways that cause harm to our families. He calls that "sin." The wonderful thing is, like Joseph, He willingly forgives and helps us and our families become healthier. What a God!

Families are still messy today. How can we deal with our messes? Read the story of Joseph in Genesis 45-48, and consider what Joseph did to help his family begin the healing process. We each can contribute to the healing of our families, often by simply forgiving, as Joseph did.

Pray that someday, your family will be a real meat sandwich instead of that soupy mess... and give thanks if you already have a healthy family.

Prayer: *God who has forgiven me of much, thank You. Guide me to forgive, as Joseph did, and help my family move beyond the mess we have.*

"To forgive is to set a prisoner free and discover that the prisoner was you." Lewis B. Smedes

"Forgiveness is the fragrance that the violet sheds on the heel that has crushed it." Mark Twain

"God recycles evil into righteousness." Max Lucado

"Your mess will become your message." Max Lucado

"Nothing in this lost world

Bears the impress of the Son of God

So surely as forgiveness has."

Alice Cary

MULTIPLY LIKE RABBITS

Genesis 8:15-20 (NIV)
¹⁵ Then God said to Noah, ¹⁶ "Come out of the ark, you and your wife and your sons and their wives. ¹⁷ Bring out every kind of living creature that is with you—the birds, the animals, and all the creatures that move along the ground—so they can multiply on the earth and be fruitful and increase in number on it."

A couple of months back, when I would walk around the condo building where I live, there would be cottontail rabbits around, nibbling and feeding in the late evening, just before dark. Yesterday, I was out just before dusk, and there were families of cottontails all around. Two put on a show for the four or five of us who were out getting a refreshing change from our isolation during the coronavirus pandemic. They were jumping a couple of feet into the air, defending their territory, not desiring another family in their green spot.

Then an eagle flew over and the rabbits disappeared. Disputes were forgotten; protection was more important. I've always wondered how all the animals got along in Noah's ark, what kept the eagles from eating the rabbits, the lions from eating the lambs, the robins from eating the insects. That's a question for when I get to heaven.

Yet when I think of Noah and all those animals, I am amazed. I'm amazed at how God chose to protect them, provide adequate food (did some hibernate?), and even provide food when they got off the ark onto dry ground. I'm amazed that Noah and his family had the energy to feed them all! I'm amazed that when they got off the boat, they didn't fight or dispute over territories until they had adequately "multiplied."

Then I think back to Adam and Eve and their sons Cain and Abel. Those two boys had a dispute. They didn't wait until "multiplication" had occurred. Cain was jealous of Abel, so he just killed him. It sounds like the animals did a better job of following God's commands than Cain did. But then, their examples of Adam and Eve weren't too good either. They had disobeyed God, and trouble had started.

Isn't the same true for us? Animals follow the plan God has for them. Even though we often don't like to look at one species eating another species, it is in the plan God has to keep balance in the world. But we as humans want to take things into our own hands, do our own thing. We disobey the plan He has designed for us because it doesn't agree with what we plan and want. I've discovered the hard way that I am not fruitful, and that I don't multiply spiritually when I seek my way first, and I sure don't multiply in helping other people come to know Him.

Wouldn't it be wonderful if we would all "multiply and grow like rabbits" in love, joy, peace, gentleness, and self-control?

Prayer: *Lord, help me to look to You for aspects in my life where You want me to "multiply and grow like rabbits" so that I may be more like You.*

"Prayer is how God gives us so many of the unimaginable things He has for us. Indeed, prayer makes it safe for God to give us many of the things we most desire. It is the way we know God, the way we finally treat God as God. Prayer is simply the key to everything we need to do and be in life." Tim Keller

NO NAIL TO HANG HIS HAT ON

Matthew 18:20 NIV
"Jesus replied, 'Foxes have dens and birds have nests, but the Son of Man has no place to lay his head.'"

I have so many questions I'd love to have answers for. Do you? One thing I'd like to know – did Adam and Eve sleep on the ground, or make a bed of leaves? Did they ever create a tent? Another thing – how did Abraham and Sarah deal with the elements in their nomadic lifestyle? Moses and the Israelites roamed for 40 years in the wilderness. Did they have tents? Was the hot desert sun beating down on them constantly? And David seems to be a rags-to-riches kind of guy – living in caves, later moving to a palace. Was it a hard adjustment? Many of our Biblical friends had no nails on which to hang their hats.

Some better questions might be: How would I have treated them? The same way I treat homeless people today? And for today's homeless population, what am I doing for them? Am I teaching those capable to fish, or throwing a fish to them from a distance? Or ignoring them? For those mentally unable to work, do I treat them with the respect that Jesus would give them? Do I avoid them as if they are lepers?

Tough questions for middle class people like me - who like to be comfortable, want people to smell good, want to contribute to a church or an agency that will take care of them... not do something for them personally. Oh, I have some good excuses – my compromised immune system, my fears, other things God wants me to do – but what does God want me to do? What is my responsibility when it comes to giving them a nail on which to hang their hats?

Prayer: *Lord, I need an attitude adjustment. I don't want it. I'm comfortable as I am. But I'm not acting like You. Guide me as only You can guide me – transform my mind, so I am more like You. Thank You.*

"We think sometimes that poverty is only being hungry, naked and homeless. The poverty of being unwanted, unloved and uncared for is the greatest poverty. We must start in our own homes to remedy this kind of poverty."
Mother Teresa

Luke 12:12-14 ESV

[12] He said also to the man who had invited him, "When you give a dinner or a banquet, do not invite your friends or your brothers or your relatives or rich neighbors, lest they also invite you in return and you be repaid. [13] But when you give a feast, invite the poor, the crippled, the lame, the blind, [14] and you will be blessed, because they cannot repay you. For you will be repaid at the resurrection of the just."

NO NEWS IS GOOD NEWS

Isaiah 52:7 International Children's Bible (ICB)
⁷ How beautiful is the person
who comes over the mountains to bring good news.
How beautiful is the one who announces peace.
He brings good news
and announces salvation.
How beautiful are the feet of the one who says to Jerusalem,
"Your God is king."

Isaiah 61:1-3 New International Version (NIV)
61 The Spirit of the Sovereign Lord is on me,
because the Lord has anointed me
to proclaim good news to the poor.
He has sent me to bind up the brokenhearted,
to proclaim freedom for the captives
and release from darkness for the prisoners,
² to proclaim the year of the Lord's favor
and the day of vengeance of our God,
to comfort all who mourn,
³ and provide for those who grieve in Zion—
to bestow on them a crown of beauty
instead of ashes,
the oil of joy

instead of mourning,
and a garment of praise
instead of a spirit of despair.
They will be called oaks of righteousness,
a planting of the Lord
for the display of His splendor.

Growing up, I often heard my mom say, "No news is good news." She was referring to something she had not had an update on, something that she was assuming had turned out OK. She believed that if there was bad news on the subject/person, she would have been notified.

News. We can have it 24/7 if we so choose: Internet, 24-hour news stations on the radio and TV, newspapers, magazines, and the list goes on. But most of it is not good news. Much of it can make us depressed if we focus on it. We may find relief in the human-interest stories that seem to be the only source of good news on many stations.

But good news is easy to access. Today's scriptures are chosen from the Old Testament, and foretell of the birth of the good news that is announced in the four gospels that are at the beginning of the New Testament, Matthew, Mark, Luke, and John. That good news is that we can be assured of eternal life by simply believing Jesus. Oh, the story often sounds like bad news – after all, He was hunted as a child with the intent to kill (and many others were killed trying to find him), He was severely mistreated as an adult, and crucified to death, the cruelest form of death known to man at the time. His followers were depressed, anxious, and scared. Then a few people began to see the man who had died that horrible death walking around, and they even could see His scars. That was good news! Good news that was welcomed and that those folks began to talk about. The government could not make them be quiet. They tried, but when you are that excited, it is hard to keep your mouth shut! In fact, we Christians are still talking about it, two thousand years later! The idea is hard to grasp, but then many worldly ideas are also hard to understand - like the idea that life sprang into being without a Creator. One gives great hope. The other has no good news attached for me. So I choose the one with the hope, the peace, the assurance. I hope your choice is the same.

***Prayer:** Jesus, You are good news! And we'd rather have good news than feel that we have to wait and watch wondering if the news will be good or bad. Thank You for being available to all of us and for helping us have assurance of Your love and our salvation. Thank You for the story of Your life in the four gospels at the beginning of the New Testament, and for the knowledge that we are not waiting to know if "no news is good news."*

"Religion can be one of the greatest hindrances to faith because it creates dependency on a ritual rather than on the God of the universe who can do all things."
Tony Evans

OPENED A CAN OF WORMS

Judges 16:4 New International Version (NIV)
⁴ Some time later, he fell in love with a woman in the Valley of Sorek whose name was Delilah. ⁵ The rulers of the Philistines went to her and said, "See if you can lure him into showing you the secret of his great strength and how we can overpower him so we may tie him up and subdue him. Each one of us will give you eleven hundred shekels of silver."

Did you ever go cane pole fishing? That was the only way we knew how to fish when I was growing up in the panhandle of Florida in the 1940's-60's. One of the first things to do in preparation was to go to a compost/manure pile and dig down to get wigglers and earthworms and put them into a can. We would then take them to the creek and use those wigglers to bait the hooks of our fishing poles. Those cans of worms were dirty, ugly, and full of wiggling worms all tangled up together, wanting to escape, but unable to crawl up the side.

Almost everyone has heard the story of Samson and Delilah. Chapters 13-16 of the book of Judges tell us quite a bit about this man, Samson, whom God chose to do some of His work. This story is an excellent example of

God using someone who has problems and doesn't live an upright life to complete some of His work. It also includes a good example of "opening a can of worms" and getting dirty, wiggling around, and wanting to crawl out of the prison Samson had created for himself.

If you recall this story, Samson was dedicated to the Lord at birth by his parents, Manoah and Mrs. Manoah (Judges 13). He was to be a Nazarite, did not cut his hair, and would deliver Israel from the Philistines. For the most part, Samson lived a life following the rules he needed to follow to be a Nazarite, but he loved the ways of the world, and hanging out with prostitutes was apparently his favorite pastime. Today, if he were living, we would say that he had an addiction to sex. It would get him in trouble, but like a pornography or drug addiction, he never seemed to learn that it would lead to trouble over and over again. So he fell for Delilah. What a can of worms!

Delilah apparently didn't fall for him, but instead fell for silver. As the story goes, she was to be paid big money to get him to tell her how he was so strong that he could tear down buildings and destroy lions with ease. So she would continuously try to get the info from him. He lied to her a few times, then gave in and told her the truth. While he slept, she cut his hair. He was captured, and she got her silver. You can read through chapter 16 for the rest of the story if you don't know it.

Not too smart, but then I've done many dumb things in my life. I might be opening another can of worms if I criticize him!

What a mess addictions can get us into. They open many "cans of worms." When we feel the need for sex, drugs, alcohol, shopping ventures, gambling, or other addictions more than we feel the need for self-control or for God, it has control over us. It will lead us to a filthy mess of tangled up worms, with no apparent way to get it all straightened out. But like Samson, when we begin to obey God, we regain our strength, those worms escape and go back to their normal environment, and life smells a lot sweeter.

I love this story because it tells me that God can use any messed up human being for His purpose, and that He wants messed up people like me to work on straightening out the tangled up worms in our lives.

***Prayer:** Lord of the tangled messes, who can repair relationships, heal broken families, and wash away the filth, we come seeking to see our weaknesses, and the desire to begin to untangle the worms in our cans. We can't do it alone. We need Your Holy Spirit to work with us so we can overcome and be instruments of light for You.*

"An intelligent person can rationalize anything, a wise person doesn't try." Jen Knox

"Don't magnify your problems, magnify your God... He's got you covered." Tony Evans

OTHER FISH TO FRY

John 21:1-14 International Children's Bible (ICB)

21 Later, Jesus showed himself to His followers by Lake Galilee. This is how it happened: ² Some of the followers were together. They were Simon Peter, Thomas (called Didymus), Nathanael from Cana in Galilee, the two sons of Zebedee, and two other followers. ³ Simon Peter said, "I am going out to fish."

The other followers said, "We will go with you." So they went out and got into the boat. They fished that night but caught nothing.

⁴ Early the next morning Jesus stood on the shore. But the followers did not know that it was Jesus. ⁵ Then He said to them, "Friends, have you caught any fish?"

They answered, "No."

⁶ He said, "Throw your net into the water on the right side of the boat, and you will find some." So they did this. They caught so many fish that they could not pull the net back into the boat.

⁷ The follower whom Jesus loved said to Peter, "It is the Lord!" When Peter heard him say this, he wrapped his coat around himself. (Peter had taken his clothes off.) Then he jumped into the water. [8] *The other followers went to shore in the boat, dragging the net full of fish. They were not very far from shore, only about 100 yards.* [9] *When the followers stepped out of the boat and onto the shore, they saw a fire of hot coals. There were fish on the fire, and there was bread.*

[10] *Then Jesus said, "Bring some of the fish that you caught."*

[11] *Simon Peter went into the boat and pulled the net to the shore. It was full of big fish. There were 153. Even though there were so many, the net did not tear.* [12] *Jesus said to them, "Come and eat." None of the followers dared ask Him, "Who are You?" They knew it was the Lord.* [13] *Jesus came and took the bread and gave it to them. He also gave them the fish.*

[14] *This was now the third time Jesus showed himself to His followers after He was raised from death.*

Research on the background of this idiom is that it has been used since the 1600s, implying that the person has something more important to do. Sometimes it is used as "bigger fish to fry," and refers to the person having something more important to do.

If you've ever been to Israel, you know that much of the shoreline of the Sea of Galilee is rocky, high above the water. In the places where the shoreline is accessible, it is like a small beach on a large lake in America. This is where I picture Jesus cooking fish, talking with His disciples, after surprising them with both His presence and a big catch of fish.

Those disciples had a choice. They could take the fish and go off to the market to get money to provide for their families. They could stop and have breakfast with Jesus (fish is still eaten for breakfast in Israel today.) They could sell the catch and use the money to buy a new boat, gamble, or a multitude of other things. They could have even given the fish away. They chose time with Jesus. They chose the right fish to fry.

When you and I have fish to fry, what is our choice? Time with Jesus? Family? Fun? None of these are bad things, but one brings you the greatest joy and peace.

Prayer: Lord, I'm tempted to take care of my desires and wants, to please my family and friends, and to ignore You. Forgive me. Those are not the best of the fish. Help me ignore the distracting fish and choose You as the best.

"Men, God is not opposed to greatness. God is opposed to pride. Big difference. Unfortunately, it is a difference not widely understood or embraced." Tony Evans

"Change your thoughts and change your world." Norman Vincent Peale

"The reality is that the Lord never calls the qualified; He qualifies the called." Henry Blackaby

PAY PEANUTS, GET MONKEYS

> *1 Corinthians 6:19 The Passion Translation (TPT)*
> *¹⁹ Have you forgotten that your body is now the sacred temple of the Spirit of Holiness, who lives in you? You don't belong to yourself any longer, for the gift of God, the Holy Spirit, lives inside your sanctuary.*

Wow, my body is God's temple! It amazes me that He lives in me. I am in awe when I think of this, and how He lives in each of us who trust Him as our Savior and Lord.

And yet, I've taken this body for granted. For years, I've paid peanuts to take care of it, not thinking about the consequences of inadequate nutrients, exercise, and sleep. I've overeaten sugar and undereaten greens. I've skipped sleep to overwork. I've thought parking on the far side of the parking lot and walking across it would get me adequate exercise. Wrong. Peanuts got me monkeys. I now deal with a type of blood cancer and many other issues. Was this because of how I took care of my body? I don't know, but I suspect it was a factor.

Yes, I know there are others who have also not taken care of their bodies, and so far have not suffered consequences.

And I also know that there are people who took care of their bodies and yet suffer from major health issues. So yes, there are other factors, including genetics and environmental issues, that can play a part in someone developing serious health problems. Still, the truth remains that we need to care for the bodies that God has given us.

Now I need to pay big dollars to take better care of this temple of the Holy Spirit. It needs some good deep cleaning, just like my home needs an annual spring cleaning. But thank God for the drugs that are wiping out cancer cells even if they cost a lot more than peanuts!

> **Prayer**: *Lord, lead each reader of these words and me to make better choices regarding the care of Your temple. Help us understand the connection between how we treat our bodies and the things that will happen in years to come. Help us understand that paying peanuts will only get us monkeys.*

"He who has health, has hope. And he who has hope, has everything." Benjamin Franklin

"A healthy outside starts from the inside." Robert Urich

"Your body is a temple, but only if you treat it as one." Astrid Alauda

PRACTICE MAKES PERFECT

Hebrews 12:11-13 J.B. Phillips New Testament (PHILLIPS)
¹⁰⁻¹³ For our fathers used to correct us according to their own ideas during the brief days of childhood. But God corrects us all our days for our own benefit, to teach us His holiness. Now obviously no "chastening" seems pleasant at the time: it is in fact most unpleasant. Yet when it is all over we can see that it has quietly produced the fruit of real goodness in the characters of those who have accepted it in the right spirit. So take a fresh grip on life and brace your trembling limbs. Don't wander away from the path but forge steadily onward. On the right path the limping foot recovers strength and does not collapse.

Practice makes perfect – or does it? I've questioned this many times. For example, a person following a recipe might decide that two cups of flour would be better than one. The resulting cake would not be what she wanted. She's practiced making a cake, perhaps over and over, but practicing didn't make it perfect because she didn't practice <u>correctly</u>. Practicing holding a tennis racket correctly takes many small steps of coaching and encouragement to finally master it so that it is perfect. If the player keeps doing it the way that starts off feeling natural, they will never master it. Discipline is needed in order to get to the point that it is "perfect."

Living life is the same. Practicing the same things over and over without small increments of change creates a habit that is not perfect. It's true with relationships, it's true with finances, it's true with housekeeping, and it's even true with becoming more godly. These things don't just happen. We make small increments of change until we get to the point that we are doing these things right. We may be corrected by a parent, a coach, a teacher or we may learn to correct on our own – self-discipline.

Take filing, for example, since it is something I don't like to do. If I deal with the mail every day, toss the junk mail, scan the important things I want to keep, pay bills immediately, and neatly file anything I need to answer in a tickler file, it doesn't overwhelm me. But if I let it stack up, it gets overwhelming very soon! I had to learn to make changes in how I dealt with mail in order to find what I needed when I needed it.

Yes, developing godliness via the fruit of the Spirit (love, joy, peace, patience, kindness, generosity, fidelity, tolerance, and self-control) in my life is the same. I may fail at patience, but I can gradually develop it by practicing it for longer and longer periods of time, with different issues, and setting change as a goal, while relying on the Holy Spirit to coach me. The same is true with self-control. I may think that I can't stop eating something, but if I cut back one bite at a time, it's surprising what I can do! One bite becomes two, two bites become three, and eventually, I realize that I'm satisfied with just one or two bites, and those last bites when I'm too full don't really taste good – it's just compulsive eating. I grow in godliness, one small step at a time. As the scripture above says, I need to "forge steadily onward." I am so thankful for the Holy Spirit that is readily available to help me "forge onward."

***Prayer**: Lord, I need Your Holy Spirit as a coach so I grow in godliness, and am not stuck practicing imperfection, which does not lead to the end goal. Only practice with incremental changes for the better will help me reach perfection. Thank You, Holy Spirit, for living in me and helping me become more godly as I cooperate with You.*

"There are far better things ahead than those we leave behind." C.S. Lewis

"Think of all the beauty still left around you and be happy." Anne Frank

"Understanding the difference between healthy striving and perfectionism is critical to laying down the shield and picking up your life. Research shows that perfectionism hampers success. In fact, it's often the path to depression, anxiety, addiction, and life paralysis." Brene Brown

PRETTY IS AS PRETTY DOES

1 Kings 19:2 (NLT)
So Jezebel sent this message to Elijah: "May the gods strike me and even kill me if by this time tomorrow I have not killed you just as you killed them."

<u>Proverbs 31:30 - 31 NIV</u>
Charm is deceptive, and beauty is fleeting; but a woman who fears the Lord is to be praised. Honor her for all that her hands have done, and let her works bring her praise at the city gate.

When I was a child, if I did something I should not do, invariably one of my parents would say to me, "Pretty is as pretty does." I heard it from teachers, my grandmother, my aunts… and since I liked to please people, I aimed to "do pretty" for them.

Jezebel strikes me as a woman of wealth and beauty, able to have all the best of the makeup of that time to make her skin glow, her eyes look as if they were set deep in her head, and long eyelashes batting to get the attention of the men. Something worked. She got attention.

But she didn't do pretty. She killed prophets. She killed Naboth so her husband could have his vineyard.

She commanded elders and townspeople and they listened to her, probably out of fear. They didn't want to be killed. Her actions weren't pretty, her attitude was not pretty, and her relationships weren't pretty. Yet, she was a leader to whom people paid attention.

Contrast her with Mary, the mother of Jesus. She was humble, probably wore no makeup, and was the mother of several children, including some likely rambunctious boys as they grew up. When she told the servants to do what Jesus said, they respected her – a healthy respect, not one of fear of death. They did it, and the people had wine at the wedding feast, at which she likely was assisting in some way. (See John 2:1-11.)

You and I have choices. We can be pretty on the outside but not so pretty on the inside. Or we can constantly work with God to be transformed on the inside, so that we become more like Him, thus pretty on the inside. As the proverb says, beauty is fleeting. But pretty on the inside brings honor. God rewards a good attitude.

Prayer: Lord, help me recognize areas where I need to grow to be more like You. Make me pretty on the inside, no matter what I look like on the outside. Help me be more spiritually healthy in You, so that people will see the beauty that only You can give.

"A woman's heart should be so hidden in God that a man has to seek Him in order to find her." Anonymous

Proverbs 31:30 The Message
Charm can mislead and beauty soon fades.
The woman to be admired and praised
is the woman who lives in the Fear-of-God.

RUNNING AROUND LIKE A CHICKEN WITH ITS HEAD CUT OFF

Mark 4:35-41 The Passion Translation (TPT)
40 Then He turned to His disciples and said to them, "Why are you so afraid? Haven't you learned to trust yet?" 41 But they were overwhelmed with fear and awe and said to one another, "Who is this man who has such authority that even the wind and waves obey Him?"

"The hurried-er I go, the behinded-er I get" was one of my mom's favorite quotes. Do we ever have an example of Jesus hurrying? I can't think of a time when He hurried.

As a child, we had chickens. When it was time to fry a chicken or to make chicken and dumplings, mom would select the right pullet or grown chicken, grab it by the neck, and wring it until the neck was broken. Some people chopped the head off instead of wringing the neck. The nerves continued to work for a few minutes, and the chicken continued to move. It would flop around until surrendering to death. When anyone described a person in a particular situation as "running around like a chicken with its head cut off," everyone familiar with the chicken's reaction had a mental picture of the frenzy the person was experiencing.

In the passage above, Jesus was sleeping, probably on the floor of the boat withno pillow or blanket, when a bad storm came up. His disciples were afraid for their lives, running around like "chickens with their heads cut off." What did He tell them to do? Trust.

When I hurry, I typically am afraid something is not going to get done, or that I'm going to let someone down. What is Jesus's answer to my fear? Trust! When I do, I relax, slow down, and quit "running around like a chicken with its head cut off." I feel more joy, contentment, and peace. It's not always easy, but it is always worthwhile.

Hurrying is not the same thing as working fast with our hands, or running/walking at a speed that is healthy for us. Hurrying involves rushing to get a job done, not paying attention to the quality of the work many times, and perhaps striving to please someone by completing the task. I find that it helps to take a deep breath or two, assess the work, be sure that my attitude is one of trust in God to get me through the task, and trust in the work quality when completed. We will feel much better and no longer feel that we need to describe ourselves as "a chicken with its head cut off."

***Prayer:** Lord, teach me to trust. "Running around like a chicken with its head cut off" does not show trust, and I'd rather be focused on You and putting my trust in You to get me through the tasks at hand. Help me to do my work with accuracy and with appropriate speed, but not with hurry and rushing. Thank You.*

"Never be in a hurry; do everything quietly and in a calm spirit. Do not lose your inner peace for anything whatsoever, even if your whole world seems upset. What is anything in life compared to peace of soul?" Francis de Sales

"In our rushing, bulls in china shops, we break our own lives." Ann Voskamp

STUBBORN AS A MULE

1 Kings 10:25 (NIV)
Year after year, everyone who came brought a gift—articles of silver and gold, robes, weapons and spices, and horses and mules.

James 3:3 (NIV)
³ When we put bits into the mouths of horses to make them obey us, we can turn the whole animal.

My dad was a farmer. As a young man, if you had given him a mule, it would have been like giving him a big fancy tractor in this day and age. He would have thought he was living "high on the hog." Solomon may have felt just as great about the mules brought to him!

As a child, I remember Dad behind a mule, with a plow, cultivating the land. I also have fond memories of him hitching the mule to a wagon, and we would ride into town to get a few supplies or go to the gristmill with a bag of corn to be ground into meal for our cornbread. In hindsight, I doubt it was a comfortable ride – I recall a board across the wagon as the place we sat. It was hard, had no cushion, and the ride was rough. There was no protection from the elements – sun, rain, wind, sleet, or whatever came our way. But it was faster than walking and not as tiring.

The mule was usually cooperative, but since it was a mule, it was not always! Sometimes it didn't want to move. Other times, it wanted to go faster than was safe. That's why there was always a bit in its mouth when it was supposed to be working. That little bit could be used to control the mule just as horse riders still use them to control their horses. The animal understands it and realizes what he is supposed to do. His mouth is comfortable as long as he obeys, but as soon as he rebels, he is uncomfortable enough to be motivated to obey.

In James chapter three, James, the brother of Jesus, talks about teachers needing to live up to higher standards than others because they are role models, and then he transitions to tongues, and their need to be under control. He uses the comparison of the bit in the horse's mouth. I confess, I'm stubborn like a mule at times, and I don't want that bit in my mouth. I want to spit out all the self-control I have and say what I think. The trouble is, when I do that, I get myself in trouble. But unlike a stubborn mule, there is not a carrot, apple, or trough of hay waiting for me. Instead, I suffer regret, damaged relationships, and I may hurt someone's feelings. The truth is that I'm so much better off with the bit of self-discipline in my mouth! I'll bet you've learned the same thing but perhaps, like me, you need to keep re-learning it. Thankfully, the lessons can grow further and further apart as we practice holding that stubborn mule of a tongue!

Prayer: God, Who created me, help me learn to control my tongue. Teach me the self-discipline I need to keep from saying things that I will regret. I don't want to be "stubborn as a mule."

"Self-discipline is doing what needs to be done when it needs to be done even when you don't feel like doing it." Anonymous

"Without self-discipline, success is impossible, period." Lou Holtz

Proverbs 5:23

For lack of discipline they will die, led astray by their own great folly.

TAKE MY MARBLES AND GO HOME

Philippians 2:3-4 World English Bible (WEB)
³ doing nothing through rivalry or through conceit, but in humility, each counting others better than himself; ⁴ each of you not just looking to his own things, but each of you also to the things of others.

James 4:1-2 GOD'S WORD Translation (GW)
⁴What causes fights and quarrels among you? Aren't they caused by the selfish desires that fight to control you? ² You want what you don't have, so you commit murder. You're determined to have things, but you can't get what you want. You quarrel and fight. You don't have the things you want, because you don't pray for them.

Marbles – those little glass orbs with sparking colors – were a game that children played frequently when I was a child. Children often had a small bag of them that they carried in their pockets so they could play anytime, anyplace. All that was needed were a few marbles, a spot of dirt, and at least one other child. But children then were children – and the attitude of many was competitive - to win at any price! Thus the saying developed, "take my marbles and go home" when a child could not win and got angry about it.

But that attitude existed long before marbles and will last long after marbles, because children (and adults) are competitive, and we want to win, and that can bring out a selfish part of us. I like what James (who, incidentally, was the brother of Jesus) says in the verses above: "What causes fights and quarrels among you? Aren't they caused by the selfish desires that fight to control you?" Yes, my selfish desires fight to control me, and unless you are superhuman, yours do too!

We see it in board rooms, in churches, in professional sports, among celebrities, in social groups, in gangs, and in families. When one of us puts our needs and wants ahead of everyone else's, if the others don't go along with it, that person may "take his marbles and go home."

Paul tells us in Philippians to "not look at our own interests but at the interests of others." When we each consider the needs of others before being pushy and demanding our own way, life is much more pleasant, and the rewards of working cooperatively with others include peace. We are each happier.

Does Jesus want me to "take my marbles and go home?" If it is because of selfishness, then the answer is "no." He certainly is not an example of "taking His marbles and going home." He chose to accept abuse and punishment for me – there is nothing selfish about that! I suspect His marbles are all still in His pocket, ready for a game when we get to heaven.

Prayer: Thank You, dear Jesus, for Your example of unselfishness. Help me remember as I work and play with others to always be willing to share, to put their interests ahead of mine, and to never "take my marbles and go home" because of a selfish attitude.

Philippians 2:3-4 New International Version (NIV)

³ Do nothing out of selfish ambition or vain conceit. Rather, in humility value others above yourselves, ⁴ not looking to your own interests but each of you to the interests of the others.

"Selfishness is not living as one wishes to live, it is asking others to live as one wishes to live." Oscar Wilde

"Every man must decide whether he will walk in the light of creative altruism or in the darkness of self-destruction." Martin Luther King

THE DEVIL IS IN THE DETAILS

Luke 4:1-2 New International Version (NIV)
⁴ Jesus, full of the Holy Spirit, left the Jordan and was led by the Spirit into the wilderness, ² where for forty days He was tempted by the devil. He ate nothing during those days, and at the end of them He was hungry.

This German proverb likely started as "God is in the details." Somehow, it got changed and was used in the 1960s by German architect Lugwig Mies van der Rohe. It became a popular saying in the 1990s, especially among business people.

No matter what translation or paraphrase I read the above scripture in, the fact remains that Jesus was tempted all forty days He was out in that wilderness. I never noticed that little detail until recently, but it's always been there. I knew He was out there for forty days, and I knew the three temptations shared with us in verses later in the chapter, but He was tempted every day for forty days!

Does it matter? Absolutely! Because every day, I'm tempted. My Savior experienced what I experience – daily temptation. In fact, it doesn't make sense that He was only tempted three times in 40 days. He would not have been fully human if that had happened. He couldn't identify with me if He was not fully human.

Yes, the devil is in the details. He (Satan) wanted me to think that Jesus was not fully human and put doubt in my heart. He wanted me to believe Jesus could not identify with me. But he was wrong. Jesus, You win!

Prayer: Lord, forgive me that I ignored that little detail all those years. Show me other details as I need to see them, that Your truth may be totally revealed to me. I trust You. Thank You.

"Do the right thing. It will gratify some people and astonish the rest." Mark Twain

"I follow three rules: Do the right thing, do the best you can, and always show people you care." Lou Holtz

THE EARLY BIRD GETS THE WORM

Mark 1:35 (NLT)
³⁵Before daybreak the next morning, Jesus got up and went out to an isolated place to pray.

Romans 8:28 (NLT)
²⁸And we know that God causes everything to work together for the good of those who love God and are called according to His purpose for them.

I'm an early bird. I was married to a night owl. God made us both and loved us equally, but that didn't make it easy to agree on when to do things!

Jesus was an early bird too, and as we see in this passage, He used early morning to pray. When the apostles found Him that morning, He was ready to go to work! Basically, He said, "Let's go to some of these other little towns around here. They need to be taught, so let's go do it." He was ready. He had risen early and talked to God about the plans for the day. He was at peace, He knew what to do, and He knew when to do it.

If you are ever up early in the morning, you see birds flitting about. In the area where I live, the earthworms often crawl out onto the pavement or sidewalks. Mockingbirds can be seen checking for them and grabbing them for a high protein breakfast. In the winter, they compete with the robins to get to them first. Truly, it is the early bird that gets the worm.

God made us each unique, and it doesn't make one more godly to be up early, but it does make one more godly to plan and work with God on what should be done during the day. In fact, this is true throughout life, no matter what time we arise. Sometimes, He changes our plans mid-course, and sometimes, life gets in the way and thus our plans are changed in the process. We often don't see the good in those times of change until long past the event that created the change, but eventually, we realize that God has kept His promise – things do work out for what is best in the long run.

***Prayer:** Lord, I'm glad to be an early bird, to enjoy Your sunrises, and the freshness of the morning. But I'm far more thankful that things work out for what is best, and that I can always be confident that they will work out for what is best. Your plans will not go awry, and when life gets in the way, You still will work things out for good – and I will learn and grow. Thank You.*

"An hour of planning can save you ten hours of doing." Dale Carnegie

"Prayer should be the key of the day and the lock of the night." George Herbert

"Do not have your concert first and tune your instruments afterward. Begin the day with God." James Hudson Taylor

THE SQUEAKY WHEEL GETS THE GREASE

Luke 18:1-8 (NLT)
¹Jesus told them a parable, about how they should always pray and not give up.

² 'There was once a judge in a certain town,' He said, 'who didn't fear God, and didn't have any respect for people. ³ There was a widow in that town, and she came to Him and said, "Judge my case! Vindicate me against my enemy!"

⁴ 'For a long time he refused. But, in the end, he said to himself, "It's true that I don't fear God, and don't have any respect for people. ⁵ But because this widow is causing me a lot of trouble, I will put her case right and vindicate her, so that she doesn't end up coming and giving me a black eye."

⁶ 'Well,' said the master, 'did you hear what this unjust judge says? ⁷ And don't you think that God will see justice done for His chosen ones, who shout out to Him day and night? Do you suppose He is deliberately delaying? ⁸ Let me tell you, He will vindicate them very quickly. But – when the son of man comes, will He find faith on the earth?'

Can you imagine the pioneers driving their covered wagons cross country, listening to a squeaky wheel, constantly fearful that robbers would hear them and come after them? Or a stagecoach full of passengers moving cross country with a constant squeak? Maybe your car has a sound. Likely, you are quick to try to figure out why, where, and what can be done to stop it. Or perhaps it's a leaking faucet that is driving you crazy with the sound of that drip-drip-drip. We don't like listening to things that don't seem normal or right. The pioneers would have had some type of oil or grease with them to put on that squeaking wheel. Farmers travel the fields with it too, just in case the equipment needs a quick adjustment.

We can be just as prepared. We can talk to God about any worry or any nagging thoughts that we have. It doesn't matter if they are injustices, as the lady in the parable of Luke 18 was dealing with, or a health issue, or a financial issue, or a relational issue, or a salvation issue, etc. God will listen. And He keeps on listening. Sometimes He is slow to answer, and sometimes I'm slow to recognize His answer. Sometimes He has it answered before I finish expressing it. And sometimes, He says "No." After all, He sees the long range, the future. I only know the here and now. His wisdom is far greater than mine. He may be teaching me to trust Him, to wait, to be patient, to love unconditionally, or anything else He wants me to learn. But I can be assured that peace will come, no matter what His answer. I can also be assured that He wants me to talk to Him about it.

The same is true for you. He wants you to talk to Him, no matter what the situation. This little story tells us that about Him, and that is an important thing to know about the God of the universe.

Prayer: Thank You, listening God, that You care enough to assure me that You always have a listening ear, that You are better than any human judge. You love me, even when I'm as irritating as a squeaky wheel. Thank You for consistently providing peace as a part of Your answers.

"God can handle your doubt, anger, fear, grief, confusion, and questions. You can bring everything to Him in prayer." Rick Warren

"Prayer is the greater work." Oswald Chambers

"God speaks in the silence of the heart. Listening is the beginning of prayer." Mother Teresa

1 Kings 8:28

Yet give attention to Your servant's prayer and his plea for mercy, Lord my God. Hear the cry and the prayer that Your servant is praying in Your presence this day.

TWO WRONGS DON'T MAKE A RIGHT

Proverbs 4:26-27 Tree of Life Version (TLV)
²⁶ Clear a level path for your feet,
so all your ways will be firm.
²⁷ Do not turn to the right or to the left.
Divert your foot from evil.

John 8:32 New International Version (NIV)
³² Then you will know the truth, and the truth will set you free."

If I had a nickel for every time I've heard, "Two wrongs don't make a right," I'd have hundreds of pounds of nickels. How many times have we tried to make ourselves look good after making a mistake by making an excuse, telling a "little white lie?" For many of us, it becomes a habit in our childhood that is hard to break in our adult lives. After all, we want to look good!

But is it wise? The Good Book tells us not to be diverted toward evil, but away from it. Galatians 1:10 tells us to be God pleasers, not people pleasers. As I face those situations, who am I caring the most about? Pleasing the other person, pleasing God, or looking good? Probably I am caring most about looking good, and therefore, I'm being selfish! Is it better to be acceptable in the eyes of God or in the eyes of man?

Years ago, I had an experience where I had a tough decision to make. I thought I had made it, but suddenly the thought came to me, "If I do this, I will have a lot more difficult moments ahead." I knew I'd not please one particular person who wanted me to do wrong, and that it would create conflict. And then, a peace washed over me as I realized that if I was going to do what was right, I had no choice but to just do it. So, difficult moments did come, but what blessings have resulted! My life has been so much better as a result of those tough times and decisions. I have no regrets about them.

No, two wrongs don't make a right. May I remember this and may you remember it as we face those times when we want to look good, or perhaps want to avoid conflict.

Prayer: Lord God of truth, we come to You acknowledging that there is frequent temptation to please people and to look good. But truth sets us free, and we want freedom. We know that sometimes pleasing You leads us to other tough times, but we also know that in the long run, we are so much better off. Two wrongs never lead to better times, only to more little white lies, if there is such a thing.

"You cannot make yourself feel something you do not feel, but you can make yourself do right in spite of your feelings." Pearl S. Buck

"Remember not only to say the right thing in the right place, but far more difficult still, to leave unsaid the wrong thing at the tempting moment." Benjamin Franklin

Psalm 106:3 NIV

Blessed are those who act justly, and always do what is right.

UP THE CREEK WITHOUT A PADDLE

Genesis 37:23-24 New International Version (NIV)
²³ So when Joseph came to his brothers, they stripped him of his robe—the ornate robe he was wearing— ²⁴ and they took him and threw him into the cistern. The cistern was empty; there was no water in it.

Genesis 37:28 New International Version (NIV)
²⁸ So when the Midianite merchants came by, his brothers pulled Joseph up out of the cistern and sold him for twenty shekels of silver to the Ishmaelites, who took him to Egypt.

Genesis 45:4-5 New International Version (NIV)
⁴ Then Joseph said to his brothers, "Come close to me." When they had done so, he said, "I am your brother Joseph, the one you sold into Egypt! ⁵ And now, do not be distressed and do not be angry with yourselves for selling me here, because it was to save lives that God sent me ahead of you.

Genesis 50:15 New International Version (NIV)
¹⁵ When Joseph's brothers saw that their father was dead, they said, "What if Joseph holds a grudge against us and pays us back for all the wrongs we did to him?"

HOMESPUN DEVOTION

Recommended reading: Genesis 37-50

The meaning of this idiom is simple – we're in trouble! We have an awkward predicament, or perhaps a **serious** situation. It was likely first used in the military when a soldier was lost. But it could be a lot older – back to the time of Joseph! Poor Joseph was up a creek without a paddle, multiple times. Then his dad also had a difficult predicament – to send his other son Benjamin to Egypt, or starve. When Jacob, Joseph's father, died, the brothers feared they would be the butt of Joseph's anger, and felt they were up the creek without a paddle.

If you don't know this story well, I encourage you to read it from beginning to end. It is a beautiful story of forgiveness, and you may have seen it in a movie or a play (Sight and Sound Theaters usually do it annually.) But it's more than a story of forgiveness. It shows repeatedly that when we are in difficult predicaments, we can turn to God, and He will direct us to a paddle that we can use to canoe right on out of the mess we are in.

Jeremiah quotes God with "I know the plans I have for you." Paul states that things will work together for our good. Sometimes it doesn't seem like good is going to happen, but it does. Think about this teenage boy, Joseph. He foolishly bragged about his dreams to his brothers, and since they were already jealous of him because their father played favorites, they created a scheme to kill him, but decided instead to sell him. While he was down in that pit, and later following along behind that wagon train as a tied up slave, he was likely feeling as if he was up the creek without a paddle. But God had a plan for him, turned it all into good, and saved a family in the process. Not just a family, but THE family that would be the ancestors of Jewish people today, and from which Jesus was born.

The dad decided to risk sacrificing his other favorite son, Benjamin, in order to keep his family alive. Again, he felt like he was up the creek without a paddle. But a family was saved as a result of that decision, and good came from evil.

And those boys with the guilty consciouses grew up to be men with guilty consciouses. They schemed up a lie in order to try to save their lives, thinking they were up a creek without a paddle. But they didn't have to worry – God used that boy they sold into slavery to hand them a paddle, and they were able to be free because of the forgiveness He offered them.

This is a great example of God's love for us - His willingness to rescue us when we are in times of trouble. I can think of multiple times He has rescued me. Likely, you can too.

Prayer: Lord, I create my own messes. I get lost up the creek, with no paddle to help me get home. Thank You for the hundreds of times You've rescued me, even more that I don't recall, perhaps never even realized. Honestly though, I'd rather not get lost, so help me stay on the path or creek You have designed for me. Help me learn as I go, and not make mistakes I've made in the past. If I do get lost, provide me with the paddle I need. Thank You.

Jeremiah 29:11 New Revised Standard Version Catholic Edition (NRSVCE)
"For surely I know the plans I have for you, says the Lord, plans for your welfare and not for harm, to give you a future with hope.

Romans 8:28 New Revised Standard Version Catholic Edition (NRSVCE)
[28] We know that all things work together for good for those who love God, who are called according to His purpose.

Psalm 86:5 New International Version (NIV)
[5] You, Lord, are forgiving and good,
abounding in love to all who call to you.

WAKE UP AND SMELL THE COFFEE

Proverbs 19:11 International Children's Bible (ICB)
[11] A wise person is patient.
He will be honored if he ignores a wrong done against him.

Luke 9:51-56 Holman Christian Standard Bible (HCSB)
[51] When the days were coming to a close for Him to be taken up He determined to journey to Jerusalem. [52] He sent messengers ahead of Him, and on the way they entered a village of the Samaritans to make preparations for Him. [53] But they did not welcome Him, because He determined to journey to Jerusalem. [54] When the disciples James and John saw this, they said, "Lord, do You want us to call down fire from heaven to consume them?"

[55] But He turned and rebuked them, [56] and they went to another village.

Attitude is a choice. I'm working hard to have a good attitude as I watch the news and see the things going on around me. Last week, a Minneapolis police officer was documented while holding his knee on an African American man's neck for nine minutes. The man died. This week, as I write, there are protests (legal) and riots (illegal). Many of the riots are causing fires, and people are stealing and doing other illegal things. Why? Yes, from all the evidence, the policeman and fellow policemen did not do what they should have done. I understand the anger. I feel the anger to some degree, but not as my African-American friends do. But let's all "wake up and smell the coffee" and while realizing that "two wrongs don't make a right," let's work to overcome these and all the other injustices with compassion and love.

I am reminded of the golden rule found in Matthew 7:12, "So, in everything, do to others what you would have them do to you, for this sums up the Law and the Prophets." Yes, it is a great summary, and we would have a peaceful world if all of us practiced it.

When I look at the children's version of the verse quoted from Proverbs above, I find that wise men often ignore the wrongs done against them. That is what Jesus did, concerning the town in Samaria that did not welcome Him. His apostles wanted to call down fire to consume (kill) the people, but He was quick to tell them "No" and move on to a more welcoming place. He ignored the wrong done to Him.

Can I do the same? Can I be compassionate and loving as I would want others to be with me? Can I work to mend relationships among different ethic groups? Jesus loves everyone equally – He has no favorites, so why do some of us seem to assume we are His "teacher's pets?" Am I afraid of people just because they look different? Jesus was not, so I need not be. In fact, there is wisdom in not judging a person based on their ethnicity. I've got some work to do –

changing my attitude and being sure I treat all people with compassion and love.

Prayer: Lord, You don't favor me over a person from another country, another ethic group, another skin color, or another religious belief. You love each of us the same, unfailingly, unconditionally. You show compassion and You issue justice with mercy and love. You teach us to treat others as we want to be treated. I need to be more like You. Change my attitude and lead me to "wake up and smell the coffee" anytime I fail to show compassion and love.

"Violence never brings permanent peace. It solves no social problem: it merely creates new and more complicated ones. Violence is impractical because it is a descending spiral ending in destruction for all." Martin Luther King, Jr.

I Peter 1:22 NIV

[22] Now that you have purified yourselves by obeying the truth so that you have sincere love for each other, love one another deeply, from the heart.

WAS THE JUICE WORTH THE SQUEEZE?

> *Isaiah 41:10 New Life Version (NLV)*
> *¹⁰ Do not fear, for I am with you. Do not be afraid, for I am your God. I will give you strength, and for sure I will help you. Yes, I will hold you up with My right hand that is right and good.*

The origin of this phrase seems to be unknown, but it has been used for centuries. Sometimes, you hear it as "The juice ain't worth the squeeze." I prefer the more positive approach as a question. Basically, it is asking if the results are worth the work. Is the orange juice worth the work of squeezing the oranges?

Sometimes life squeezes us. For example, as I write this, I am isolated. I'm usually an outgoing people person, but for health reasons, I need to stay away from gatherings for several months. Chemotherapy compromises your immune system, and mine is already compromised. I don't want the flu, a stomach virus, tonsillitis, and especially COVID 19. So, the best thing to do is to take the doctor's advice, and stay home. That's hard for a life-long teacher who loves to be in the limelight.

But I believe that the juice is worth the squeeze. God is God, He is sovereign, and He is upholding me with His right hand – and I will go through these months, and be a healthier person on the other side. I will grow in the fruit of the Spirit, and I will find blessings daily as I feel the squeeze. I will use the time productively to do things I've postponed and procrastinated on. This time away from family, friends, and church family will be a blessing. I'll appreciate each of these more after the extended time as well.

Prayer: Lord, You assure me that You will strengthen me and uphold me. I'm counting on You to teach me the lessons I most need to learn as I walk through this time of isolation. I have faith that You will make the juice worth the squeeze.

"God will make good out of this mess. That's His job."
Max Lucado

WHEN IT RAINS, IT POURS

Job 1: 18-19 NLT
¹⁸While he was still speaking, another messenger arrived with this news: "Your sons and daughters were feasting in their oldest brother's home. ¹⁹ Suddenly, a powerful wind swept in from the wilderness and hit the house on all sides. The house collapsed, and all your children are dead. I am the only one who escaped to tell you."

Most of us know the story of Job. If not, we likely are familiar with the phrase, "the patience of Job." The verses above are after Job has lost his oxen, donkeys, sheep, camels, and his servants. Can you imagine Job, hearing one disaster after another, and how overwhelmed he felt, how sad, how rejected and alone, and how empty? He likely wished that they had taken the sword to him as well. It was not just raining for Job. It was pouring.

A few years ago, I knew a lady who suffered many catastrophes in her life. Her house burned down to rubbish. Soon thereafter, her daughter (only child) died in an automobile crash. Within a month, her husband died of a sudden heart attack. The aunt for whom she was caretaker, committed suicide. She herself was diagnosed with lung cancer, stage four. All of this happened in about three months. She was overwhelmed, felt rejected, alone, empty, sad, and wanted to die. It was not just raining for her... it was pouring.

Those of us with cancer often get a glimpse of these types of trials. For some of us, one diagnosis leads to another, leads to another, and leads to yet another. The body seems to be falling apart with things frequently going wrong. If we are not focusing on God and on those things that are noble and true, we will become overwhelmed, anxious, alone, empty, and sad – and lose our purpose for living. It takes effort to redirect ourselves, to sing God's praises instead of cursing Him, and to trust instead of fear. When your energy is limited, this seems even harder, but never is it more important! When it rains, it pours down blessings. That's a silver lining.

Prayer: *God of rain, and God of blessings, help me to look at the times when my life is flooded with health issues, troubles, and things Satan throws at me as times of great blessings, when You are at work and pouring down blessings on me – blessings I may not see, including faith, perseverance, trust, hope, and love. Mature me as Your child as I struggle to be positive in spite of the issues. Slow me the silver lining of blessings that follow the pouring rain.*

"I have always believed, and I still believe, that whatever good or bad fortune may come our way we can always give it meaning and transform it into something of value."
Hermann Hesse

"We can always choose to perceive things differently. We can focus on what's wrong in our life, or we can focus on what's right." Marianne Williamson

Romans 12:2a NIV

Do not conform to the pattern of this world, but be transformed by the renewing of your mind.

WISH I COULD HAVE BEEN A FLY ON THE WALL...

Psalm 51:6-9 (Good News Translation) GNT
⁶Sincerity and truth are what you require;
fill my mind with Your wisdom.
⁷ Remove my sin, and I will be clean;
wash me, and I will be whiter than snow.
⁸ Let me hear the sounds of joy and gladness;
and though you have crushed me and broken me,
I will be happy once again.
⁹ Close Your eyes to my sins
and wipe out all my evil.

2 Corinthians 7:10 English Standard Version (ESV)
¹⁰ For godly grief produces a repentance that leads to salvation without regret, whereas worldly grief produces death.

The Bible often lets us be "a fly on the wall," showing us the faults of the men and women in the scriptures. It is not a romance novel with almost perfect characters!

A good example is David. I Samuel 11:12 tells us about David taking sexual advantage of a neighbor lady, and that encounter resulting in pregnancy. David didn't want her husband to know, so he had him killed so he could marry this lovely lady. He went into denial about the entire situation and pretended there was nothing wrong with what he had done.

But then...

The prophet of God, Nathan, came along and confronted him. His guilt overflowed, and he wrote Psalm 51, allowing us to be a "fly on the wall" and read his thoughts. Wow, it makes me uncomfortable, and yet it is strangely comforting.

Why? His godly sorrow is so obvious that I'm a little ashamed of being in his presence, "a fly on the wall."

But then...

I'm just as guilty. Oh, not of murder of a person's body, but perhaps murder of a person's self-worth a few times in my life. And guilty of not controlling my tongue. Guilty of doing things to please others. These make me even more uncomfortable.

But then...

I can have the same peace that David found as he wrote his prayer (Psalm 51). I can feel that godly sorrow, I can pour out my emotions to God, and be washed clean, restoring my peace. Oh, I may need to apologize to whomever it was that I wronged, but I can even muster up the courage to do that because God will empower me.

And then... peace.

Prayer: *Lord, help me be willing to have a contrite heart, as David did, when I sin. Like him, I can talk to You, and You willingly provide grace and relieve me of my guilt. What a great gift! No wonder I love You. Thank You that there are stories all through Your word about people who messed up, and how You used and forgave them anyway. Thank You for being "the fly on the wall" Who shared them with us in Your Holy Word.*

Psalm 51 World English Bible (WEB)
[1] Have mercy on me, God, according to
Your loving kindness.
According to the multitude of Your tender mercies,
blot out my transgressions.
[2] Wash me thoroughly from my iniquity.
Cleanse me from my sin.
[3] For I know my transgressions.
My sin is constantly before me.
[4] Against You, and You only, I have sinned,
and done that which is evil in Your sight,
so you may be proved right when you speak,
and justified when you judge.
[5] Behold, I was born in iniquity.
My mother conceived me in sin.
[6] Behold, You desire truth in the inward parts.
You teach me wisdom in the inmost place.
[7] Purify me with hyssop, and I will be clean.
Wash me, and I will be whiter than snow.
[8] Let me hear joy and gladness,
that the bones which You have broken may rejoice.
[9] Hide Your face from my sins,
and blot out all of my iniquities.

HOMESPUN DEVOTION

¹⁰ Create in me a clean heart, O God.
Renew a right spirit within me.
¹¹ Don't throw me from Your presence,
and don't take Your Holy Spirit from me.
¹² Restore to me the joy of Your salvation.
Uphold me with a willing spirit.
¹³ Then I will teach transgressors Your ways.
Sinners will be converted to You.
¹⁴ Deliver me from the guilt of bloodshed,
O God, the God of my salvation.
My tongue will sing aloud of Your righteousness.
¹⁵ Lord, open my lips.
My mouth will declare Your praise.
¹⁶ For You don't delight in sacrifice, or else I would give it.
You have no pleasure in burnt offering.
¹⁷ The sacrifices of God are a broken spirit.
O God, You will not despise a broken and contrite heart.
¹⁸ Do well in yYur good pleasure to Zion.
Build the walls of Jerusalem.
¹⁹ Then You will delight in the sacrifices of righteousness,
in burnt offerings and in whole burnt offerings.
Then they will offer bulls on Your altar.

CAN'T HAVE YOUR CAKE AND EAT IT TOO

James 1:5-8 The Passion Translation (TPT)
⁵ And if anyone longs to be wise, ask God for wisdom and He will give it! He won't see your lack of wisdom as an opportunity to scold you over your failures but He will overwhelm your failures with His generous grace. ⁶ Just make sure you ask empowered by confident faith without doubting that you will receive. For the ambivalent person believes one minute and doubts the next. Being undecided makes you become like the rough seas driven and tossed by the wind. You're up one minute and tossed down the next. ⁷⁻⁸ When you are half-hearted and wavering it leaves you unstable. Can you really expect to receive anything from the Lord when you're in that condition?

Life is confusing – at least to me at times. Probably to you too. And when it's confusing, I don't know what to do. I want to keep my cake and I want to eat it, too. I wanted to keep my house and I wanted to sell it to move to independent living. I want to keep my integrity and I want to please people. I want to skip chemo and be healed instantly. I want to go to a big event and I want to avoid germs. Conflicting feelings, confusing thoughts.

Sometimes our wants have to be weighed and we have to determine what the wiser thing is. As James described,

"Being undecided makes you become like the rough seas driven and tossed by the wind." But he advises us on how to handle this: Seek wisdom from God! I only need to talk to God about it, and He will guide me to my next steps. Sometimes the answers are quick and clear – like maintaining integrity, pleasing God, not man, or like having the chemo so God can use it to heal me. Sometimes, I need to keep seeking wisdom for a while, such as when I was seeking the best time to move to an independent living facility. Confident faith that God has the right answer will lead me to the right decision in His perfect timing. I know this from experience, yet I too often forget.

***Prayer:** Lord, empower me with confident faith, so that I don't fight You and Your will, but seek Your wisdom and surrender to Your perfect timing. I know I can't "have my cake and eat it too." Continue to grow my trust in You as we work through the issues of life that can be so confusing.*

Proverbs 1:7 New International Version (NIV)

The fear of the Lord is the beginning of knowledge, but fools despise wisdom and instruction.

1 Corinthians 1:25 New International Version (NIV)

[25] For the foolishness of God is wiser than human wisdom, and the weakness of God is stronger than human strength.

YOU GOT THE DRESS AND THE SHOES, BUT DIDN'T MAKE IT TO THE PARTY

Philippians 3:13-14 New International Version (NIV)
¹³ Brothers and sisters, I do not consider myself yet to have taken hold of it. But one thing I do: Forgetting what is behind and straining toward what is ahead, ¹⁴ I press on toward the goal to win the prize for which God has called me heavenward in Christ Jesus.

Romans 1:13 (NIV)
¹³ I do not want you to be unaware, brothers and sisters, that I planned many times to come to you (but have been prevented from doing so until now) in order that I might have a harvest among you, just as I have had among the other Gentiles.

Have you ever made plans for something for which you were very excited, but at the last minute, you just couldn't pull it off? Ever had a goal you really wanted to meet, but circumstances put a stop to it, either suddenly or gradually? You felt like you had the dress and shoes, but you didn't get to go to the party!

Paul could have recounted that same type of thing. He had plans to go places that God redirected him away from, so he didn't go. But that's not what he's talking about in Philippians. Instead, he's focusing on his spiritual goal, and he's pressing on! He's not giving up, not "crying over spilt milk," and not blaming God for a mistake or trying to change God's mind.

How often do I focus on my personal goals, expecting to meet them? When I decided to become a master gardener, I set my timetable, took the classes, did the volunteer work, and got my certificate. Most days, I write one of these devotionals, and if I miss a day, I try to write two on another day, so that when I'm ready I can pursue publishing them. Am I that good with spiritual goals? No. Pursuing holiness and practicing godliness should be my daily goals, but I'm so easily distracted. Life gets in my way. Are you a little like me? Quite possibly.

Let's look to Paul, and remember that even though he didn't go on all his desired missionary trips, it didn't stop him from pursuing the main thing: To press on and get the prize for which God had called him.

> **Prayer:** *Sovereign God, You know how many times I get distracted from the things I most need to pursue, especially holiness and godliness. Forgive me and redirect me. When it's time for You to take me home, I don't want to just "have the dress and shoes, I want to go to the party" in heaven with You.*

> "Give me six hours to chop down a tree, and I will spend the first four sharpening the axe." Abraham Lincoln

YOU REAP WHAT YOU SOW

Galatians 6:7-8 The Message (MSG)
7-8 Don't be misled: No one makes a fool of God. What a person plants, he will harvest. The person who plants selfishness, ignoring the needs of others—ignoring God!—harvests a crop of weeds. All he'll have to show for his life is weeds! But the one who plants in response to God, letting God's Spirit do the growth work in him, harvests a crop of real life, eternal life.

Ephesians 5:16-21 Names of God Bible (NOG)
16 Make the most of your opportunities because these are evil days. 17 So don't be foolish, but understand what the Lord wants. 18 Don't get drunk on wine, which leads to wild living. Instead, be filled with the Spirit 19 by reciting psalms, hymns, and spiritual songs for your own good. Sing and make music to the Lord with your hearts. 20 Always thank God the Father for everything in the name of our Lord Yeshua Christ.

You get out of something what you put into it. The modern way of saying it is "garbage in, garbage out." Some variation of the thought, "You reap what you sow" has been around at least two thousand years, since the apostle Paul wrote it to the Galatians. He may have even heard it from somewhere else, so it could have started long before him. So yes, it is

Biblical, and tells us that God designed and planned for man to have free will, and to reap the consequences of what we do, whether positive or negative.

Paul also admonishes us to make the best of our days. He includes avoiding drunkenness, because it leads to such foolish decisions, even to "wild living." He tells us to replace our foolishness by singing songs of praise, and by being thankful. Who is the happiest, the drunk person or the one singing and being thankful? I'm thankful to say I've never been drunk, and I hope I never am, based on how I've seen drunk people behave! But I have sung and prayed, and I know that leads to a happy heart.

However, that does not mean I've not made plenty of foolish decisions and reaped what I've sown! But I've also made some good ones, such as choosing to attend college and getting my degrees, and pursuing a career that was fulfilling and that provided for basic needs.

I have the choice today to be foolish or wise, and I will reap what I sow. In most cases, I choose to eat correctly, to exercise, to get rest, because I want to maintain my health at least at the level it is, if not get better. I choose which TV shows to watch, which books to read, knowing that "garbage in, garbage out" is not in my best interest. I choose hobbies that are fulfilling but are not going to harm my body.

Yes, we do reap what we sow. Let's sow kindness, love, joy, and peace. Let's skip the wild oats and weeds and move toward plants that are cultivated to better meet our true needs.

***Prayer**: Lord, You are a God of design, of plans, of purpose. Help me live my life by Your design, and with the purpose and plans to honor You with the daily little decisions that I make, that I may reap the rewards, and thus actually sow kindness, love, joy, and peace for those who come in contact with me. Thank You.*

"There comes a time in life when you have to choose to turn the page, write another book, or simply close it."
Shannon L. Alder

"You are not the victim of the world, but rather the master of your own destiny. It is your choices and decisions that determine your destiny." Roy T. Bennett

MAY GOD BLESS YOUR HEART

As we conclude, I thank you for reading and pray you have benefited in some way. May your heart be blessed by what you have read and may the blessings below be fulfilled in your life.

> Ephesians 3:16-20 International Children's Bible (ICB)
> [16] I ask the Father in His great glory to give you the power to be strong in spirit. He will give you that strength through His Spirit. [17] I pray that Christ will live in your hearts because of your faith. I pray that your life will be strong in love and be built on love. [18] And I pray that you and all God's holy people will have the power to understand the greatness of Christ's love. I pray that you can understand how wide and how long and how high and how deep that love is. [19] Christ's love is greater than any person can ever know. But I pray that you will be able to know that love. Then you can be filled with the fullness of God.
>
> [20] With God's power working in us, God can do much, much more than anything we can ask or think of.

Numbers 6:24-26 International Children's Bible (ICB)
^{24} May the Lord bless you and keep you.
^{25} May the Lord show you His kindness.
May He have mercy on you.
^{26} May the Lord watch over you
and give you peace.

Made in the USA
Monee, IL
24 March 2021